More praise for
Making Shapely Fiction

"*Making Shapely Fiction* embodies its very title by giving form to the art and craft of fiction. It didn't take long after I peeked into this sensible and sensitive guide for Jerome Stern's music to capture me—and I read the book in a single sitting. This guy is very good!"   —Richard Lederer, author of
The Play of Words

"Jerome Stern has done us all a favor with this canny book. If you are interested in writing, *read it now*. This is an expert writer and teacher sending his notes from the trenches. Never has caution been so exhilarating, advice so wry. I will use this book."
            —Ron Carlson, author of *The Hotel Eden*

"A very useful book—and it's lots of fun to read."
            —Bill Henderson, editor of *The Pushcart Prize:*
Best of the Small Presses

"Jerome Stern's holistic approach is as practical as it is inspired. He is a spirited guide who knows the landscape and is delighted to show you around personally, providing maps and blueprints."
            —James Thomas, professor of English at
Wright State University and coeditor of
Sudden Fiction International

"*Making Shapely Fiction* clarifies the mumbo-jumbo. For serious students of fiction, Jerome Stern is the Alpha crow. Follow him and shave the miles off your flying time."   —Bob Shacochis, author of
Swimming in the Volcano

MAKING SHAPELY FICTION

MAKING SHAPELY FICTION

·

Jerome Stern

W. W. Norton & Company
New York · London

TO MAXINE AND BAYARD

First published as a Norton paperback 2000

Printed in the United States of America.

The text of this book is composed in Sabon,
with the display set in Stymie.
Composition and manufacturing by The Maple-Vail
Book Manufacturing Group.

Book design by *Guenet Abraham.*

Library of Congress Cataloging-in-Publication Data

Stern, Jerome (Jerome H.)
    Making shapely fiction / Jerome Stern.
        p.   cm.
    Includes bibliographical references.
    1. Fiction—Authorship.   I. Title.
    PN3355.S78   1991
    808.3—dc20   90-36676

ISBN-13: 978-0-393-32124-1
ISBN-10: 0-393-32124-X

W. W. Norton & Company, Inc.
500 Fifth Avenue, New York, N.Y. 10110
www.wwnorton.com

W. W. Norton & Company Ltd.
15 Carlisle Street, London W1D 3BS

20

Contents

PART II

A CAUTIONARY INTERLUDE

PART III

FROM ACCURACY TO ZIGZAG:
AN ALPHABET FOR WRITERS
OF FICTION

PART IV

READABLES: WHERE TO LEARN MORE

WHAT THIS BOOK DOES AND WHY

In introducing *Making Shapely Fiction,* I feel like the cook who keeps saying, "Taste it, just taste it. You'll like it."

This book is different from other books on writing. It's organized so that you can start writing serious fiction (or non-serious, if you like) from the first page. At the same time, it's arranged so that you can easily look up helpful explanations and clear examples of the techniques you need. The book is for people who are already writing fiction and for those who always wanted to give it a try.

"The Shapes of Fiction" part is first. These shapes aren't rules that you follow so much as ways to create. For example—you remember the smells and sensations of your childhood on an army base. You have images of gray tankers, a man in a uniform who wanted to show you his capybara, a woman making whimpering noises in a park, a blonde girl who said she was going to feed you to a snake. The "Shapes of Fiction" gives these swirling memories narrative forms. The shapes show you how they can become fiction.

The second part, "A Cautionary Interlude," consists of two short essays of general advice for writers. I wrote "Write What You Know" because it's such an unending problem. On the one hand, "Write what you know" is a tiresome platitude. On the other hand, it's an inescapable truth. I thought it would be worth reflecting upon the complexities of that phrase, "what you know," in order to raise the possibility that you know more than you think, but also less too. To write well we must let ourselves discover how much we really do know.

"Don't Do This" suggests some ways of avoiding traps and pitfalls in writing fiction. Some people can put a great deal of time into a story that for one reason or another might be doomed from the start. The don'ts are meant to tell people about such things and perhaps save them some time and disappointment. On the other hand, some people love traps and pitfalls, and to them, the don'ts will be read as challenges. No problem there. One person's cliché is another person's breakthrough. But fair warning's been given.

The third part is the most important. The "Alphabet for Writers of Fiction" might seem a strange way to organize information, but it came out of a recognition about writing fiction. Science studies have a clear order. You learn elements in Chapter 1 that you need to understand for Chapter 2, and so on. Performance arts also start with learning basic techniques, the steps or the scales, and each stage grows from a mastery of the one before.

But writing fiction doesn't have any clear hierarchy. You can't say that you must understand plot before dialogue, description before point of view, or even beginnings before endings. There's no rational order or sequence in which those elements must be learned. They're *all* necessary.

Not only that, they're never learned in the sense of being mastered or solved. They're constantly being relearned, reconsidered. Each piece presents its own problems. A common experience is to write a story that works pretty well. That success gives a pleasant confidence that's dashed in the next story, which turns out to be a multi-limbed mess. In the first story you probably had a natural shape that kept you from problems you didn't know you couldn't handle. The second story presented those problems—that's when your education as a writer really began.

Techniques of fiction, though they can be given different names, aren't really separate from one another. Henry James perceptively noted that he couldn't think "of a passage of description that is not in its intention narrative, a passage of dialogue that is not in its nature descriptive, a touch of truth of any sort that does not partake of the nature of incident." In other words, good description advances plot, dialogue reveals character, and ideas cause emotions. Nothing is just one thing. The essays in this book always refer to other entries that deal with related matters.

Another feature of the "Alphabet" is that while you're looking something up, an essay related simply by the accident of the alphabet might strike your eye, and that might supply some information you didn't know you needed.

I've cited works that are instructive and make good examples, generally staying with fairly well-known writers. Often I make reference to Gustave Flaubert's *Madame Bovary*. (Some might think, too often.) But that novel is indispensable because it's so full of complicated, subtle, and useful technical maneuvers, devices, tactics, and strategies. *Madame Bovary* isn't just a fine novel—it's a writer's handbook.

But the liveliest way to explain techniques, terms, or problems, I found, was to make up my own scenes and stories. That way I could make sure the examples were clear and to the point. But more important, I wanted to communicate the joy of writing, the sense of play that can free your thoughts, open you up to possibility. I want the book to be fun to read. I think you'll learn more, remember more, and come back more often for advice and inspiration.

After the "Alphabet" is a part called "Readables." It contains useful, helpful, or interesting works that I wanted to tell you about.

I'm somewhat skeptical about the oft-heard admonition "Write, right now." I worry that it's a little like saying "Ski, right now." For the person who's been skiing for a while it's fine advice—"Put down your damn toddy and get out in the snow." To a person who's never skied before, it's a bit smug. You might want a map, instructions, and decent equipment before you start down hill.

Making Shapely Fiction is the guide that I hope writers of fiction will carry with them for reference, for encouragement, and for some new angles on old slopes.

ACKNOWLEDGMENTS

I would like to remember my teachers: Howard Shaw at the Bronx High School of Science, who unknowingly inclined me toward literature; patient Vernon Harward at the City College of New York, who sent me toward Chapel Hill; and C. Hugh Holman of the University of North Carolina, who was always kind, no matter what he really thought. I thank my friends of the English Department at Florida State University who provided advice and encouragement. I owe a deep debt to my students, who watched these ideas develop, and particularly Allen Woodman, who kept telling me I ought to write this book. The Novel Seminars, Primary Sources, and La Colazione were a continual source of insights. I thank Dan, Jesse, Linda, and Pete for their reactions and suggestions on the manuscript. And last, I'd like to express my gratitude and admiration for Carol Houck Smith, a teacher's teacher, and an editor's editor.

PART I

THE SHAPES OF FICTION

▼

◯ A shape invites you to fill it. The shapes of fiction inspire by presenting ways to embody your experiences, memories, and imaginings. Some of these shapes are particularly suited to the creation of individual scenes, short stories, or single chapters. Others could be extended to develop entire novels.

The shapes form a sequence. Each will help you with the ones that follow. The first three, *Facade, Juggling,* and *Iceberg,* show how to handle thoughts, dialogue, and action—techniques you'll use over and over. The next two, *Last Lap* and *Trauma,* concern ways of beginning short stories. *Specimen, Gathering, Day in the Life,* and *Onion* explain how to form awkward material into focused narratives. *Journey, Visitation, Aha!*, and *Bear at the Door* are the natural shapes that are at the heart of almost all fiction of any length. *Snapshot* shows how to transform a visual technique into narrative form. *Blue Moon* tells how to make fantasy or improbability convincing. *Explosion* suggests ways of testing the limits of fiction.

Each shape closes with cross-referencing to the "Alphabet for Writers." I put the cross-references at the end of each essay since I didn't want to interrupt your reading. You might want to look at these entries while you're reading about a particular shape.

▼
FACADE

○ For this technique, tell an anecdote in the voice of a character who is *not* you. But as the character tells his story have him unknowingly undercut or discredit his explanation.

For example, our character, Shroub, tells the story of an argument he had with his roommate about whose fault it was that the cat threw up on the carpet. Shroub is explaining how irresponsible his friend was, and how he should have noticed it before it dried. But the more Shroub talks, the more garbled and excited he gets, and we realize it was Shroub who accidentally let the cat get out to eat grass that morning. We begin to sympathize with the roommate and believe that Shroub is unconsciously denying his own responsibility. Not only can we see through his story, we can see through Shroub, and realize he's the kind of person who distorts events without even knowing it.

Facade is the first shape because it focuses on creating characters through their own voices. You want your people to live on the page, but you can't make them live by writing *about* them. Readers need to hear the characters speak for themselves.

Length of sentences, choice of words, sources of images, amount of repetition—all help create character.

> McKivey came over to the house and said let's get going, don't ask no questions. I had about two dollars, grabbed what my mama calls my little thin jacket—where do you think you're going in that, she says butting in, and I say, so long, we're out of here. So I say what happened was entirely McKivey's fault. I didn't take no knife or nothing with me, just that little thin jacket and the two dollars.

You want your readers to think, I could hear that person talking. The more you capture the rhythms of speech, its hesitancies, its phrases, its long, winding, run-on sentences, and its non-sentences, the closer you come to the feel of a real person. You've made the readers believe in the character. You don't have to be grammatical or correct if your speaker isn't. The character is talking, not you. Let that distinctive voice come through.

Facade is also our first shape because it creates tension. A story doesn't happen unless there is some problem, some oddity, some incongruity. In this shape the discrepancy between the image the character wants to project and what actually comes across creates tension.

This way of creating character isn't a trick exercise. It goes on all the time. Friends, enemies, and cosmeticians try to make us see things their way. But we don't always believe them. We try to see through their words.

In order to embed information so that readers see more than the character, you have to have your character tell anecdotes with rich detail.

Suppose you have Morgan telling a story about what an admirable person his mother was, but you want your readers to realize that Morgan's mother was not so wonderful:

> I would always run the bath for Mama. She was so tired from trying to get the maid to do what she was supposed to, and Mama said I was the only one who could get the water just right, and she let me bring in her fluffy bathrobe. Daddy said he was too tired from work, but Mama said that was all right we could do fine without him, and I did her back better than he did.

Even if Morgan interprets Mom's behavior one way, readers have enough specifics to make their own judgments.

Facades can be parts of stories or stories in their own right. You don't even need a listener. (Actually, it may get in the way to have another character say, "What happened then?" or "Uh-huh" or "Really?") You don't even need to establish a setting. Voice alone can create the story.

See *Character, Dialect, Dialogue, Frame Story, Tension, Voice.*

▼

JUGGLING

○ When you have your character do one thing and think about something else not only do you create tension, you create character. *Juggling* means the way you go back and forth between action and thought to create immediacy, tension, and character.

For example, your character is Loretta, the performer. It's a dangerous act—Loretta juggles hatchets. They're shiny and sharp, with hard hickory handles; if she doesn't concentrate, she can be badly hurt. But, though she's tossing them in the air, she's worrying about how to afford the nursing bills for her father. And that reminds her of when she was a little girl, and had collected four cans of bacon grease for the war effort, and her father had told her, "You're a little soldier." Meanwhile we're nervous about those tumbling hatchets.

Make readers feel the physical immediacy of the action itself. Use an action you can describe authoritatively. Let's turn to another example. A man named Streater, for instance, is visiting a childhood skating pond. If Streater is fulfilling an old wish by ice-skating across a lake, you need to know enough about ice-skating and what natural lake ice looks and feels and sounds like to make readers feel the sensations.

That physical world has to be rendered in detail and interwoven throughout the story. If you push Streater onto the ice in the first paragraph, then drop into his thoughts for several pages, and don't return to the ice until the last paragraph, the forward motion and the immediacy of the action evaporate, and the momentum is lost. Interweaving thoughts and action keeps the story going, makes the reader feel physically there. If the character is cold and wet, keep the reader cold and wet.

Going into a character's mind gives you enormous freedom. The human mind can think of an amazing amount in seconds—memories with the sharpest of details, images and sensations separated by years, voices from the past and fantasies for the future. A paragraph of thoughts ranging over decades can occur while a shoelace is being tied. Streater, out on the ice, might be recalling an argument with his brother many years ago or a recent puzzling conversation with a good friend. Streater might not even know why he is having these thoughts and be puzzled by them. But we now feel we know Streater as well as he knows himself.

There are some techniques that you must be aware of in writing a story with this structure. One is how to go back and forth between the actions and thoughts of your character. It's relatively easy to slide from an external action to an internal one, like this:

> Streater looked down at the old skates. The blue leather cracked and lined. The laces frayed. Damn. Nothing stayed the way it should. Not Elayne, not the house, nothing. He leaned down and pulled the laces to see if they had rotted. One snapped off right at the top eyelet.

In the first sentence the narrative voice puts us behind the character's eyes. The next phrases are what the character sees. The next ones are what the character thought, and the last two slide out of the character's thoughts to describe action, what the character does. In a couple of phrases we've learned of a complicated life involving specific and general disappointments, and now we want to know more. You do not have to say "he thought" every time your character thinks, though you'll often do that as another way of moving between thought and action. People don't usually think within quotation marks, so they're best avoided.

Give your character something interesting and active to do, something that requires mental concentration and physical effort. If you have elderly, frail Maria trying to dig a yellow-jacket nest out of her tomato patch, readers will be highly attentive. But tension is not generated merely by danger. If Maria's pride and dignity are dependent on her ability to take care of herself despite her age, her efforts to thread her embroidery needle could create great tension. If the action is important to the character, then it will feel important to readers. Or, conversely, as in the story of our juggler, you create tension if the character should be concentrating, but distracting thoughts and memories intrude.

This technique does not limit itself to any particular type of story or way of seeing the world. It can have serious or humorous intentions. If a surgeon is thinking about his argument with the Mercedes mechanic while he is performing a triple bypass, readers feel both a queasy sensation and some satirical purpose.

Tension can be generated by the trials of ordinary life—a character looking for a gift in a snobbish store, or trying to unravel a borrowed fishing reel. You'll see how positively readers react when they recognize their own feelings. Actions that are fundamentally passive, like sunbathing, don't work very well. It's true that sunbathing has a goal. There are even dangers and pitfalls (will he burn? will the clouds cover the sun?), but those fears don't exactly energize the story.

When you move between action and thought, your readers are simultaneously outside and inside. That interplay is at the heart of fiction.

See *Flashback, Immediacy, Interior Monologue, Point of View, Stream of Consciousness.*

▼
ICEBERG

◯ Write an argument in which the characters' real feelings are not fully expressed. Arguments are central to fiction—they create tension and reveal character. But what your characters *don't say* can be most important.

Dialogue is often cryptic. When people are at odds, they don't necessarily say so. They can be full of anger but be unable to speak of it directly. A character might hate living in Utah or believe her brother took some of the family silver, but she'll complain about how musty the house smells. What is repressed creates tension. For example:

Brian thought, Oh God, here it comes. My Principal. The
Pig That Walks Like a Man. "Hello, sir. What a fine day."
    Eiswold nodded. "What's that on your tie, boy? Your
lunch?"
    "Oh goodness," Brian said, "I hadn't noticed. Thank you
sir."

**You can move smoothly between talking and thinking, whether
you're writing in third or first person.**

Myrtice thought if Cass showed her his gold trophy one
more time she'd stuff it up his nose. "I'd love to," she said.
"I never did get to read the inscription."

Or:

"Yes," I said. "Yes sir." As long as I kept saying that, I
knew I was safe even though I had no idea what Professor
Daroop was trying to tell me.

**It's also possible to let the reader know what both characters
are thinking.**

Caroline smiled. "Nice day. You going out to the beach?"
Caroline hated being nice to Mr. Mosely. She always thought
of him as "mister," though he was no older than she was.
He'd buy two dollars' worth of gas, and then dawdle at the
register fiddling with the Chiclets display
    "Nope. Going to the hardware store." Mr. Mosely
straightened the little packets of gum, and tried to think of
something to say. He could feel her annoyance but for some
reason he could not figure out, he wanted Caroline to

approve of him. He wanted her to see that he was an interesting person.

Dialogue is not just quotation. It is grimaces, pauses, adjustments of blouse buttons, doodles on a napkin, and crossings of legs. When people communicate, they communicate with their faces, their bodies, their timing, and the objects around them. Make this a full conversation. Not just the words part.

The argument itself shouldn't take place in a spatial vacuum. Where people talk is important. In a Jenn-Air-equipped kitchen? In the restaurant at the Metropolitan Museum of Art? Setting is like another character.

Don't give your character speechlike lines that are merely designed to provide information. Let the exposition run through the character's mind, and keep the dialogue natural.

> Caroline thought, He's one of those hang-around guys. No wife anymore, no kids in town. I've had them before. The next thing, he'll be asking me if he could sweep up or something—"Not for the money," he'll say, "just to help out." No way, buster.
>
> Mr. Mosely stopped at the door and turned. "You know, I used to work in a gas station."

Conversations are like icebergs—only the very tops are visible. Most of their weight, their mass, their meanings are under the surface. Make your readers feel the tension between what is above and what's below, and you'll have a story.

See *Atmosphere, Character, Dialect, Dialogue, Mise-en-scène, Point of View, Tension.*

▼
LAST LAP

◯ *Last Lap* places the character, right in the opening lines, close to the climax of a series of events. So the story begins partway up the face of the cliff and not when your character, Arnold, first got interested in mountain climbing.

Because Arnold is already in action, the story has immediate tension. You can introduce memories of incidents that occurred months or years ago. Arnold's childhood fascination with the pitons and the carabiners in his dad's Abercrombie & Fitch catalogue, his childhood nightmares of his parents as angry mountains, his muddy panic when he went out with his Pennsylvania college's spelunking club, his fantasies of wearing Sherpa clothing as he studied at the University of Virginia Law School library, his continued secret reading of Spiderman in his law office—all can be contained within this shape, as he makes his way up the crevices in the rock. You have the tautness of the short story with the latitude of longer fiction.

As mentioned in *Juggling,* fiction lets you slow time. A single movement of reaching over to the next handhold can take an entire page. That slowing down of time not only gives a sense of the action's significance for Arnold, but allows readers to experience the action more vividly. Cinema adopted this fictional device when it learned to use slow motion, freeze frames, and flashbacks to give emotional resonance to important scenes. Now, when it turns up in fiction, people tend to feel it as "cinematic."

To generate forward movement as the character comes closer and closer to some point, go back and forth between the present line of action (climbing the cliff face) and the flashbacks (the incidents that brought Arnold to be doing this). The flashbacks can be a sentence or two, a paragraph, or a little story within the story, though very long flashbacks tend to make readers wonder what happened to Arnold dangling up there on the cliff.

You can put your character in the midst of a bankruptcy proceeding or an apple harvest, or at the end of a marathon. Whatever it is, certain principles seem to hold. Have action that involves movement and effort. A story about a woman trying to spear a fish will be more kinetic than one about a diver who spends the whole story just waiting her turn. Make the flashbacks vivid anecdotes. Establish that the outcome is important to the character. Suggest that there are consequences, even if the character doesn't fully understand them.

All kinds of surprises and ironies are possible within the *Last Lap*. When Arnold gets to the top of the cliff, he feels an unaccustomed joy, and he shouts out like a child playing Tarzan.

See *Beginnings, Flashback, Immediacy, Suspense, Tension.*

▼
TRAUMA

◯ Write a story that starts with a traumatic event. The opening lines could be the catastrophe itself or its immediate aftermath. The event could be the death of a friend, a Dear John letter, an overflowing septic tank, or a fall into a ravine. A story could begin:

> "I'm sorry but I really have to ask you not to call any-more," Yvonne said, and hung up. She had sounded as if she were talking to a misbehaving child in her class.
> Wardle couldn't make his hand unclench the receiver.

If you start with a traumatic moment, readers are intrigued. As in *Last Lap,* you have the chance to embed background information. Wardle could recall his last date, at the skating rink, when he pompously lectured Yvonne on the permissiveness of public education. His thoughts could go back to when he was seven years old, and his mother would call him "my little lawyer" and say that "the girls had better watch out," and he always wondered what that meant.

At the same time, move the story forward. Characters reveal themselves by how they react when they're upset. Does Wardle head to a bar to order tequila shooters? Does he go to the Museum of Modern Art to meditate on the Lachaise nude in the sculpture garden? Does he memorize Latin phrases from *Black's Law Dictionary*?

Move on and keep interweaving the past. The pitfall of this shape is in making it too retrospective. After the opening jolt, can you just have the story sit there while someone mulls over the past? Generally, no. There are stories that start with a corpse (literally or metaphorically) and the rest of the story is how it happened. There are stories in which the character wakes up in a hospital bed in multiple traction. But the success of the story lies in immediacy. If the story seems to be happening right there, it will work. If it seems to be a remote reminiscence, it won't. It will feel static, and readers will itch for the character to "do something."

The events of the past work best as specific anecdotes, as flashbacks in the mind of the character. Readers should be able to hear Wardle's mother saying, " 'A,' of course you got an 'A.' What else should my boy get?"

A character in an upset state can be a powerful observer. Wardle now notices how his voice sounds whiny and demanding. Long-forgotten memories return—a little girl in ninth grade calling him a "total craphead." Derailed by his trauma, he'll do things that he ordinarily would not: Wardle walks into the Starlite Cocktail Lounge ☆☆20 Girls 20☆☆.

You don't have to bring your character to a decision or a resolution or even to arrive at some major insight. A trauma generates its own energy. Readers want to know how it happened and what happened next, and that can create a story.

See *Character, Exposition, Flashback, Intrigant, Premise.*

▼
SPECIMEN

◯ Write a story telling one anecdote about a memorable character.

People you've met are a rich source for your fiction. However, writing about your saints or monsters, clowns or heroes, turns out to be much harder than you might expect. You keep thinking, This is a terrific character, but I can't figure out how to tell the story.

Knowing too many incidents creates problems. There's the time Hubert climbed to the top of the Little River suspension bridge and did King Kong imitations, and the time he drove his MG into the Greyhound bus station lobby, and the time he put a smoke bomb in the teachers' lounge. But many incidents don't necessarily form a satisfying story. The story needs a shape.

Choose (or invent) a single incident that is particularly revelatory, a *Specimen*. It should dramatize not just what the character does, but who he is—what could be going on inside him. You might tell a particularly hair-raising anecdote, like the time Hubert tried to get into the bank through the sewer system, but if the story stays on the surface of the action, what will readers come away with except the sense that this was a very wild guy? It might be better to tell about the time Hubert stole a major chemistry exam for a friend, but wouldn't look at the exam himself, even though he was weak in chemistry too. That incident seems more evocative, and indicates a character of some complexity. The bank incident seems more exciting, of course, but it has to be told in a way that is similarly revealing.

You have to ask: What kind of understanding do I have of this character? Do I know enough about Hubert's family and background to say more than he did this and he did that? Do I have the empathy to guess what went on in his head, how he thought and felt about what he did, and what he believed he was doing? And, how do I get that into the story?

A character comes out of a dense cultural, social, and psychological matrix. The more richly this is suggested, the more resonant the portrait. Evocative details about the person's family, childhood incidents, intimate moments—all are clues that help us understand the character. And remember, too, that you're writing fiction; you're creating art. Actual facts are your raw material, not your boundaries.

The story will focus on a single main action that will provide tension, immediacy, and feeling. That means creating a setting, inventing dialogue, describing action, and rendering thoughts. While Hubert's stealing the exam, he's remembering last year, when his history teacher told him he'd probably end up in a state penitentiary.

Point of view makes a difference. For example, if you wanted to tell about an elderly woman who tried to convert the next-door family to her faith in Baha'i by bringing over wild strawberry jam and pictures of foreign children, the point of view is everything. To a busy parent, the story might be about an interfering, spooky old lady. To the child, the story could be of a fascinating, kindly eccentric. To the believer in Baha'i, it might be a story of her attempt to bring some life to a sad, sterile household.

If you write the story from the point of view of the memorable character, it forces you into imagining and rendering her thoughts and emotions rather than simply saying what the character did and said. A third-person central consciousness works well. Even more radical is doing it in first person, so that you must totally assume the voice and outlook of the character.

If you create a narrator character who tells about the memorable character, you can show their relationship, and their effect on each other. But the story must be about *both* of them. If the narrator isn't developed enough, he'll seem an unnecessary character. And if the narrator is overdeveloped, he can take over the story like a garrulous guide who won't let visitors experience firsthand what they came for.

Specimen has multiple meanings. Colloquially it's a person who's different—"He's a real specimen." Biologically it's an example of a genus, a species, a type. And the medical sense is important too. The sample in the test tube is significant; the specimen reveals what's going on, unseen, inside a person.

See *Character, Point of View, Scene, Stories within Stories.*

▼
GATHERING

○ Put a main character in a situation that draws people together—a party, a competition, a meeting, a holiday festival. For example, Rosa Ciro is a young history lecturer at the retirement dinner for Professor Clarke. She's holding a cup of red punch in one hand. She can hear the Civil War historians teasing a woman graduate student about her feminist research. The Europeanists are complaining about parking spaces. Rosa sees how the professors fondle their vest buttons and comb their hair over their bald spots. She watches the bored spouses take up defensive positions on the sofas. It's the odd, minutely specific details that make a culture vivid on the page.

Create tension by telling the story from the point of view of a character who knows the culture intimately, has been raised in it or belonged to it, but now feels alienated. In a way, she knows it too well. The strain makes her rendering of the event crackle with tension. Rosa has been an adjunct teacher for four years. She knows that most of the faculty can't stand Professor Clarke, that even if she gets her dissertation published, the department won't hire her full time because the Medievalists are plotting to get the position, and also, there's no alcohol in the punch.

Another strategy is to tell the story from the point of view of a newcomer, a stranger. The outsider can see with fresh eyes what the group accepts as too ordinary to notice. Your character could be the wife of a first-year history professor. She overhears the casual sexist jokes or notices the way the professors never listen to each other. It's important, however, that you know the group well enough to be perceptive. Whether it's a meeting of Parents Without Partners or a Cajun homecoming, if you don't know the subculture intimately, your character is likely to notice only the most obvious mannerisms, or the story will simply reveal your own prejudices.

Don't let one person or a few people monopolize the story. Let your character hear snippets of talk as well as longer conversations. Keep her own dialogue short, and don't give her any speeches that would explain the story away. How can such a story end? The event itself can supply a natural end. The character doesn't have to act out what she feels. The drama between her and her surroundings is enough for a story.

See *Local Color, Realism, Scene.*

▼
A DAY IN THE LIFE

◯ In *A Day in the Life*, the shape is created by the unit of time involved. It could be a weekend if you were writing about a guy working at a Coney Island hot-dog stand. A single day for a teacher in a ghetto school. An eight-hour shift for a hospital emergency paramedic. A few hours for a weekly poker game. Ten minutes for a usual family breakfast. Five minutes for a man who makes his living by diving from a ten-story ladder into three feet of water.

Work is a rich source for *A Day in the Life* material. What people do for a living organizes their lives and influences their personalities. Salesmanship is not just a job, it's a way of life. But other activities are also revealing—a suburban high school girl's daily trip home from school, or a single guy's Friday night at the bowling alley.

People like to know what goes on behind the scenes. Often what seems like prosaic information to you will be fascinating to outsiders. If you want to make readers experience what a morning shift in a fast-food restaurant is like, you'd describe the customer who always says, "Over easy but not too easy," the manager who checks the garbage for unused individual jellies, the graffiti scratched on the wall of the employees' toilet. Those idiosyncratic details create the feel of that life. You want to make your readers smell the grease.

Include both routine and non-routine incidents. The schizophrenic who wanders into the fast-food restaurant may be an exception to an ordinary day, but the encounter shows how things like that happen from time to time in such a job. Don't load up a story with a number of unusual events, since too much happening in a single time frame not only strains credibility, but also is false to the real nature of the routine.

This shape needs to be wound tight. Other story shapes, like *Trauma*, have a natural tension because readers wonder about what will happen next. In *A Day in the Life*, the tension must be created in other ways—in the nature of the routine itself, in its oddness or its mundaneness, in its pressure or its killing monotony, or in the conflict between the character and the routine in which she is trapped.

This last point is the most important. The central character's thoughts allow you to bring in memories, fears, and longings that are not present in the immediate time-line of the story. The woman turning scrambled eggs with her spatula always wanted to be an illustrator—she's looking at her burnt hands and thinking about working with 4H pencils and tracing-paper overlays; she's thinking about her first set of crayon pastels. The more you develop that character's thoughts, the richer the texture of the story. Readers will feel they're understanding something from the inside—not only the life, but what it feels like to live it.

See *Accuracy, Description, Realism, Texture.*

▼

ONION

○ In the *Onion,* situations take place inside situations that are within larger situations. Your characters are caught in layers of layers.

For example, Amelia is at a family wedding, talking intensely to Hugh, an attractive cousin who has caught her eye. All around her are other relatives, squealing with shock at how much the children have grown, waving paper plates heavy with giant chunks of white wedding cake, trying to drag her off to pay homage to one of the ancient immovable great-aunts. Those enveloping actions interact with your character's situation. A story of this sort could be serious or funny, poignant, or satiric. We could want Amelia to find an ally in

Hugh, or we might think she is a selfish phony. The wedding party could frustrate her plans or help them along.

Stories about families are hard to tell for several reasons. Individual histories are entangled in a complicated, shifting web of kith and kin. There are so many anecdotes to tell about so many people. As in *Gathering,* this shape brings people together. It allows readers to see the parents squabble, the uncles get drunk, the aunts flirt, the cousins sneak drinks, and so forth, all in one place at one time. When a character is named, it's easy to mention that Uncle Ted talks about nothing but his eccentric golden retriever, which apparently no one in the family has ever seen, and that Aunt Richey is believed to have once had an affair with an Italian man.

Another problem in family stories is that the point-of-view character is often passive, a person who doesn't act so much as get acted upon. In this shape your central characters have something interesting to do. We really hope that Amelia doesn't give in, as she usually does, and sing "I Believe" for the crowd. We want her to escape with Hugh.

The action in the center, as in *Iceberg,* could suggest still deeper problems. For example, at a christening, two brothers who have never resolved their real childhood resentments get into a heated argument about Florida versus California avocados. Or the action could be comic—a conspiracy of two children to get their hands on a can of beer. Or you could tell not what happens, but what does *not* happen—a young girl's failure to attract her father's attention after dressing up especially for his approval.

For this shape, it shouldn't be just one person thinking or worrying. Of course, a man at war with his salad fork at a banquet, or a teenage boy fighting with his shyness at a dance, can make a fine story, but here you want to show a person interacting intensely with someone else.

Family gatherings are full of customs—their insistence on using the King James Bible instead of "one of those heathen modern translations," their ritual denial of Uncle Savich's alcoholism. The more vividly and specifically these matters are rendered, the more interesting and engaging those layers will be. But this shape isn't exclusively for rendering families. The enveloping action could be a civil rights march, a hunt club breakfast, a religious retreat, an army advance.

Onion visualizes the shape. A center bursting with its own life is trapped in layers and layers of people. You make the slice.

See *Irony, Point of View, Showing and Telling.*

▼
JOURNEY

○ The *Journey* is the oldest, truest, most inescapable shape for a story. From nursery story to biblical narrative to contemporary novel, someone is always setting out from home.

The *Journey* doesn't need to be a literal voyage. It can start when your character enrolls in a T'ai Chi course, gets bad news from his cardiologist, or one enchanted evening sees a face across a crowded room. It can be physical or mental, deliberate or accidental, voluntary or forced, a quest or a flight. What makes it a *Journey* is that ordinary life is left behind.

Professor Zemper didn't quite know how to introduce himself to the Synovian Civic Association. Among these smiling pink jowls, who was he? He was here because he had just gotten his real estate license. Everyone said, "Join the Synovians—meet the guys with the money. If they like you they'll make you rich." But would they like someone called Professor Zemper?

"I didn't catch your name," the blond man said.

"Arthur Zemper," he said, helpless.

"Artie's his name, poker's the game," the man announced loudly to the table. "Let's play."

If you keep interweaving background information, the character grows. We understand that Zemper never finished his dissertation, having lost heart when his adviser died, that Zemper hides behind "Professor" because it disguises his lack of "Doctor," that he loves to teach, but the unpaid bills keep him awake all night.

Keep your character moving farther from his old life.

"Artie, this game is dead. Am I right? Let's you and me and some of the other guys go 'cross the river, if you know what I mean." He winked lecherously.

"Sure," Zemper said, having no idea what he meant. He tried to sound hearty. "The night is young."

The more you reveal Zemper's ordinary life, the more we understand his dislocation. If we know his day usually consists of bran flakes in the morning, a tuna sandwich at lunch, and marking freshman essays in the evening, we feel how far he is from home.

Zemper wedged himself into a seat at the crowded table. The other guys made cheerful oinking noises to show how

happy they were to be in this place. The sign outside had
said PEARL'S BIG ONES.

"Hey Artie, couple dozen oysters, right?" his new friend
said. "Man's food. Cookie, start us with the good dishes.
Blond and brunette."

A slender redhead in a sequined bikini lay across the next
table. Several men in suits leaned over her, eating oysters
from her belly. Their tongues licked her skin as they sucked
up the oysters. Zemper felt a bit sick. The girl was young.
She looked as if she could be one of his own students. Young
women he read Keats to and urged to think about the beauty
of their minds and souls.

"Wuddya think, Artie? This is the life, right? Getting any
hungry?"

One of the beauties of the *Journey* is that once you set your
character on the road, other things can happen. Unexpectedness can lead naturally to further unexpectedness. Journeys
have the logic of accident on their side.

Zemper squeezed out of the men's room door. The slender
redhead was standing in the narrow hallway toweling off
her belly.

"Hey," she smiled at him. "This place is pretty slimy,
huh?"

Zemper smiled uncomfortably.

"Guys like you don't come here much. I can tell. You're
different. A teacher or something, I bet. Could I talk to
you? My shift is over. This isn't a come-on or anything. I
did a year of junior college."

Any change that comes over the character should be implicit
in what happens. This experience makes Zemper a different
person. He sees the girl's poignancy—he feels he has some-

thing valuable to offer people, and it's not in real estate. Your readers should not be "told" about these insights or emotions but be made to feel them as the character does. Don't be afraid to let your character think about what's happening to him. But don't reduce a complex experience to a platitude or obvious moral. If the incidents are confusing, let your readers and character puzzle together.

A *Journey* need not focus on a single main character. The center of such a story (and other stories too) could be a couple, a family, even a group brought together by chance.

It's an ancient idea—life's a voyage, a pilgrimage, a trip. It's only natural that stories take this shape, and that readers like to be taken along.

See *Plot, Premise, Showing and Telling, Tension.*

▼
VISITATION

◯ If the *Journey* is the oldest story in the world, the *Visitation* may be the second oldest. It's the shape that starts with an unexpected boat pulling up on the shore, the loud knock at the door, the ringing of the phone. The visitor can be as fanciful as a talking bird or as mundane as a repairman. Whatever its origin, it is the shape of intrusion:

> Dewey was trimming rose bushes when he heard rustling from the other side of the hedge. "Yoo-hoo," a high voice said, "could I speak to you for just one little moment?"

In the *Journey* and in the *Visitation,* ordinary life is disrupted. But a visitation is a journey that comes to you:

A figure stepped through the trellis. Dewey first thought it was a girl, but it was a slender young man wearing a wide straw hat. He grinned cheerfully, waved an arm with an elephant bracelet. "Oh, dear Dewey," he said, "I'll bet you don't remember me."

The visit can be unpleasant or pleasant, comic or terrifying, annoying or promising. Visits can come from next door, from chance meetings, from political events, from internal changes, from new ideas, from distant galaxies, and from past lives:

Dewey did, when he looked closely, remember him. From a nightclub in Rome where they'd all hung out—young wiseguy Americans who survived in Italy by conning well-heeled American tourists. They'd be guides, shopping advisers, babysitters, gigolos, whatever. But this guy, Sugarman, Sweet Steve Sugarman, was famous for being totally unscrupulous. He'd even steal from the tourists' children.

"I sure could use a drink of water," Sugarman said.

The shape of this story has a natural tension. The character has been invaded.

"Oh, sure," Dewey said. "my wife'd enjoy meeting you." He hoped that phrase would signal his settledness, his happy respectability.

"A wife, eh?" Sugarman grinned.

The visitor must be intriguing, but as in all stories, readers must care what happens to your character. That comes from what you tell about him. After the petty thievery of Rome, Dewey got into minor hashish smuggling in Genoa where he was almost killed by being mistaken for someone more important. He fled to Florida and went back to school. Dewey is now a librarian, and he has almost finished a complete bibliography of all the Hardy Boys imprints.

> "Look," Sugarman said, "I need a place to stay for a couple days—a week maybe. Hotels, you know, Dewey—people look for you in hotels."

The *Visitation* can show the character conquering or being conquered, transforming another or becoming transformed—there are all sorts of possibilities. At the end, our hope might be fulfilled or might not be.

The arc of the story is shaped by the visitor. Since the story really begins with the intrusion, that probably should occur as early as possible in the narrative. Unless handled crisply, scene-setting will seem to be preface. What follows the visit also needs to be succinct or it may feel anticlimactic, as if the story goes on after it is really over.

The *Visitation* is a shape as ancient as it is contemporary. Like the *Journey*, it echoes universal experience. In a way, it is what experience is.

See *Coincidence, Plot, Position, Suspense.*

▼
AHA!

○ With this shape, a character comes to a realization. It is the shape of discovery, of disillusionment, and of revelation. It's a recurring shape in fiction because it's a natural shape in life. Your character has a certain view of the world. An incident occurs. The reaction brings about an insight.

Your character's realizations can be about other people. A child finds his mother getting terribly upset because in his picture he crayoned the sky red instead of blue. "Blue! It has to be blue! Throw that away!" The overreaction frightens the child and he begins to realize there's something wrong with her that he'll always have to watch.

Or your character's realization can be about herself; a

woman asks a salesman in a department store questions about cuff links, and the salesman's courteous answers give her an unexpected insight into the lack of kindness she has accepted in her own life.

Realizations might be about your character's past: A woman, watching a mechanic wipe his hands while he works on her carburetor, remembers something about her uncle, a brutal incident she had repressed. Realizations might be about a present situation: A broken radio on a rainy beach weekend makes a couple realize they can't stand each other anymore.

The revelations can be new perceptions, or they can involve disillusion about old perceptions. They may be sudden or they may have built up over time. Your story focuses on the incident that precipitates the recognition. Latent feelings finally come together and the character comes to a realization.

Tell the story from the point of view of the person who "realizes." Readers immediately know the thoughts and feelings of your central character, share the experience, and feel the importance of the coming-to-realize.

The precipitating incident itself could be dramatic, but it doesn't have to be. The most intense feelings might result from noticing the difference between a character responding "Oh, sure I love ya," instead of the simple "I love you."

The sequence of the story gives you choices in how to tell it. Take, for example, these events.

> Fred meets Woodrow at work. Fred admires Woodrow because he seems much more masculine and competent than himself. They go squirrel hunting together. Woodrow shoots a squirrel down from a tree, then keeps shooting it on the ground until it's nothing but bits of spattered flesh and fur.

Fred realizes there is something seriously wrong with Woodrow. They go home.

What should the first line of the story be? Should it begin with Fred meeting Woodrow at work? Should it begin with Fred at home thinking about what happened? There is no single correct answer, but basic storytelling principles can help you choose. Stories need tension and compression. If you start with Fred and Woodrow driving to the woods, or getting out of Woodrow's truck, readers have a sense right from the start that the story has begun, not that they are reading a preface. The background information about work and Fred's feelings about Woodrow are easily embedded through Fred's thoughts as he loads his gun and they begin to stalk their prey.

Another principle is that readers tend to like stories that take place in "real time." Telling a story retrospectively, after it all happened, has particular uses, but often it feels static. It distances the experience from the reader. The character is "just thinking," nothing is "really happening." If the story starts at the beginning of the hunt, the reader experiences each event with Fred, feels his shock, his confusion, and his mind working to understand what happened. If you frame stories with "I stood on the beach and remembered as if it were yesterday" formulas, you have to ask yourself if you're setting up this retrospective for a good reason, or if you're afraid to dive right into the water.

The *Aha!* is so persuasive, so pervasive, so much the basis of what feels like a story that it presents problems. You must remember, it is merely a shape, not a story. Magazine editors have a term—"Comes to Realize"—for this shape. But when a story is just another CTR it means the writer hasn't made the characters live, hasn't developed them in time and space, hasn't created an authentic setting and texture. In short, the writer has just depended on the shape and not created a world.

Unfortunately this form can also be trivialized by accepting the notion that a recognition is a solution. A sullen girl realizes that her haughty mother loved her all the time, and the haughty mother realizes that she must express her love for her sullen daughter more openly, and now all their problems are solved and they go shopping together. That simplistic psychology suits genres that require optimistic endings for problems. But serious fiction is expected to deal with complex human emotions more deeply and perceptively.

Another clichéd device in popular fiction is having the realization depend on some sort of coincidence, like a chance eavesdropping. That's not only overused, but it depends on so many coincidences that it seems contrived by the writer rather than a natural development of personality and situation.

The texture of experience is extremely important for the *Aha!* story—readers need to feel the experience, the emotions, and the insight with the character. If this story is all external detail, the realization seems to come from nowhere. If the story is all internal thoughts, the character seems to be nowhere.

Another possibility, with its own irony and power, is the story in which the reader has the realization but the character does not. For example, Cormac successfully bullies his child into signing up for Little League baseball. Cormac doesn't realize what we do—his son no longer sees him as an ally and protector, but as another enemy in a hostile world. Formally this story is much like a "coming-to-realize" story, except the realization does not come for the character within the story. There is a poignancy and open-ended quality to this strategy that is not based on mere manipulation, but on reality, on truth.

In novels, partial recognitions often lead to actions that then result in further recognitions. Detective novels are usually structured on a series of misleading recognitions until the true realization is reached, the *Aha!* that is the turning point of the novel. In short fiction, one realization can be enough. To make that moment happen is to make a story.

See *Character, Epiphany, Flashback, Interior Monologue, Scene.*

▼

BEAR AT THE DOOR

◯ Write a story in which your character has a problem:

"Henry, there's a bear at the door."

The problem should be significant:

"Henry, it's huge."

The problem should be pressing:

"Henry, I think it's trying to get in."

The story begins by establishing not only that something is wrong, but that your character has to act. Stories that begin by merely establishing that something is wrong—for example, that your character is depressed—still don't really signal whether anything will happen. A character can stay depressed for a very long time. The bear demands action. The story has already begun.

A good *Bear at the Door* will grab the reader's attention. But the problem that energizes this shape is not only the bear, the outside threat. If Henry is to deal with the problem, he has to find the bear within himself:

"Henry! Do something!"

The tension in the story comes from the battle between the challenge and the character's need to face the problem. What will Henry do? Should he try to stab the bear with a steak knife? Could he?

That conflict within the character intensifies the tension of the situation. For example: A quiet, divorced mother is told by her daughter that her second-grade teacher keeps asking her strange questions: "Does your mommy ever come home real late and leave you all alone?" "Does your mommy have a boyfriend?" "Does your mommy spank you?" The mother has to figure out what to do—for some reason the teacher seems obsessed with finding something wrong. The mother might have to take action. But she also has to fight her own distaste for confrontation.

Reactions must be in character. If the mother decides she will go to the school and speak directly to the teacher, the mother's potential for doing that has to be suggested early.

Your readers need to believe that she has it in her. Her decision shouldn't relieve the tension—it should intensify it. Now your readers have to worry whether this will make things better or worse for everybody.

In novels, problems are strung together so that solutions to one problem often generate the next problem. It is out of the frying pan and into the fire, out of the fire and into the water, out of the water and back in the frying pan, until the novel is done. In short fiction, a single problem gives the story its shape.

In certain kinds of problem stories, there are only two possibilities. The character wins or loses, hits or misses, triumphs or fails. Those stories can work well enough if they are rendered excitingly, but there is something disappointing in them, a predictability readers feel. Though readers' hearts might race, there is often a sense of being manipulated—will this be sentimental victory or sentimental irony?

Subtleties and ironies appear in the resolution when the problem and the attempted solution don't resolve themselves around a simple win-or-lose closing. The confrontation in the school might result in an impasse. The resolution might raise other questions, give unexpected insights, or be believable but strange. Henry can't pick up a knife. He puts a Mozart symphony on the stereo. The puzzled bear eats the record. Life is suggestive, not tidy.

See *Plot, Position, Suspense, Tension.*

▼
SNAPSHOT

○ Single moments—crises, revealing incidents, or epiphanies—make crisp, focused short stories. But if you're dealing with a character's whole college career, fifteen years of marriage, or an entire life in one story, it's difficult to achieve that intensity. The work is likely to seem like a sketch for a novel, a summary rather than a story. A way of retaining immediacy while covering many years is to write a series of single moments, separate in time.

Think of this story as a series of public and private snapshots, of pictures taken at crucial moments. Real photographs are silent testimonials.

A family is grouped in the driveway in front of the new Buick. The father smiles broadly, with one hand on the hood, and the other on his wife's shoulder. The two children look thin and frightened.

An older couple are sitting stiffly on a couch in a living room of French Provincial furniture. She holds up a photograph of a Lhasa Apso on her lap.

We draw conclusions about these people's taste, their jobs, their happiness. Snapshots taken over a period of time show a cute baby on a blanket, a gawky teenager in a baseball uniform, a sullen-faced young man slouched on a car fender. Each photograph is immediate, resonant with its own meanings.

The literary equivalent of the snapshot is the anecdote, the scene. Each scene is as immediate as a snapshot:

Donna trembled in the closet. She'd been playing with the crayons. She had figured out how she could make the colors go under her nails so each finger was different. Daddy had used his lawyer voice. "Go to your room. No daughter of mine is going to eat supper with fingernails like that." She stared at her bright hands.

The next scene might be days or years later; you can make sure readers quickly understand when and where it's taking place by embedding that sort of information in the first sentence or two:

Donna looked at her fiancé. Why was she doing this? She tried to get her pink corsage straight. Her father gripped her shoulder tightly. "I'm proud of you today," he said. "Joshua's a fine young man and, besides, he seems willing to put up with you." Her father smiled, as if it was a joke.

Choose evocative scenes that show what has changed and what remains the same:

Donna tried to explain to her father, "I'm not interested in support payments, I just want my half of what I can get for the house." "That's just what I thought you'd say," he said. "Just exactly."

As narrator you might stay unobtrusive, creating the scenes, and only supplying minimal information—just as a person showing an album of snapshots might say, "These are the Frontons in Sussex after Charles died," "This is Gwen's debutante party." Or you might comment freely on various characters, or tell straightforwardly how circumstances affected the history of a family, and make remarks, like "Then Gwen married this pompous little snob none of us liked. Here's a picture of him on their mahogany boat that never left the dock." Or your narrator can be reflective, meditative, and tell about his own reactions and actions. "We were all children then, but we didn't understand that. We thought we knew so much. Here's the four of us, at Sheepshead Bay, toasting our engagement."

The point, though, is to let the snapshots do most of the telling.

See *Mise-en-scène, Scene, Transitions.*

▼

BLUE MOON

◯   *Blue Moon* stories appeal to our deepest selves. We enter the world of magic, myth, and dream—fabulous characters, unfathomable mysteries, or chimerical creatures. Our sleeping world, our childhood tales, our religious beliefs are full of happenings whose reality is not of this earth.

But dealing with the unexplainable presents problems. A good story in some way changes the consciousness of its audience. If the only reaction a story can bring is "Life sure is full of mysteries," or "Gee, that's spooky," then the work hasn't taken its readers anywhere except to the reiteration of a platitude. On the other hand, Franz Kafka's "Metamorphosis," in which the main character turns into a giant beetle, gives us insight into the dark heart of modern life.

Another problem lies in our powers of imagination. In a piece of fiction you have the freedom to make up anything. You can have mermaids talking, people come back to life, misers turning into philanthropists, aliens arriving in flying saucers—all you have to do is write it down. And the trouble is, so many writers already have. There have been so many ghost stories and haunted-object stories and guardian angel stories that it is hard to be fresh and original. Readers are quick to remember early incarnations and say, "Oh, that's like another story I read." A cliché is a cliché whether from this world or the next.

Even reality presents problems. Actual events can seem too pointedly meaningful for successful fiction, such as those newspaper stories about lovers having head-on collisions as they rush to see each other, or a banker getting maimed by a falling safe—things that happen once in a blue moon. The fact that "it really happened" doesn't necessarily mean it's usable. Nature seems to have a weakness for heavy-handed irony.

So what can you do?

Fortunately, you do have something going for you. The wonderful phenomenon "willing suspension of disbelief." Readers are willing to enter whatever world you create. The question is: How can you get readers to stay in that world, and feel it as a reality? How can you repay their trust?

If you start with the sentence "There was a town, a small town, in the mountains of Carpathia where all the men were fools, and all the geese very wise," readers are likely to accept that as the premise for this world. It is the "given," and out of that given the reader will allow your story to grow. In this case you help the reader by distancing the premise in space and time. That's a useful strategy but it isn't essential. Memphis can be as magical as the mountains of Carpathia.

Another way to make the improbable acceptable is to have your narrator or storyteller acknowledge her own limitations. Your character says, "I was told this story by my grandfather when I was very young," or "I learned this from a sailor I met in Makassar." Your narrator, by not claiming responsibility for the story, adds to its credibility. The narrator is simply reporting what was told to her. Readers can believe that. And so that frankness suggests that the story itself, strange as it is, may also be true.

Readers are also likely to accept highly unusual occurrences if you warn them in advance. The narrator can indicate in the beginning his hesitancy to tell the story for fear he will be disbelieved, even laughed at. That builds the odd or mysterious events into the premise of the story. Readers know something weird will happen, so they don't feel tricked when it does. Since the narrator has confided in his readers, they have faith in the story's honest intentions.

A traditional rule of storytelling is that you can make the reader believe only one odd thing—one coincidence, one freak accident, one unusual turn of events. But suppose you want your story to be full of bizarre characters, mysterious events, outrageous coincidences, and inexplicable mysteries. Can you get readers to continue to suspend their disbelief? How do you create an unreal world that has its own logic?

Paradoxically, the answer lies mainly in the techniques of traditional fiction. Kafka's dogged detail makes his nightmare novel, *The Trial,* chillingly real. Cultural insights make

Doris Lessing's *Memoirs of a Survivor* absolutely convincing. The magic of writers like Gabriel García Márquez and Isaac Bashevis Singer feels true because of their deep understanding of human behavior. If you work on compelling characters, perceptive observations, fresh details, good prose, and shapely structures, you can create your world, and worlds beyond worlds.

See *Fairy Tale, Imagination, Legend, Parody, Premise, Romance, Suspension of Disbelief, Tour de Force.*

▼
EXPLOSION

○ Artists tend to be an unruly bunch—no sooner
do they learn their craft than they stretch the boundaries, test
their limits, find out what is really true. That's clear in modern painting. You see the young Picasso as a great classical
draftsman, and then you see him explode those techniques to
fracture his paintings into cubes, scrawls, masks, and graffiti.
In theater you see Samuel Beckett writing plays that ask: Does
a play have to be a certain length? No, it doesn't. Does a play
have to have words? No, it doesn't. Does a play have to have
motion? No, it doesn't. His *Breath* negates every convention.
In fiction, Laurence Sterne, in 1759, asked a similar set of
questions about the novel. The result was his inventive, inge-

nious *Tristram Shandy.* And writers have been exploring the conventions of fiction ever since.

Question the boundaries, test the limits, push against the edges, or turn the rules inside out. See what happens. For example, one is generally taught the following:

> Absorbing characters are the first requirement for a successful fiction.
>
> In general, stories should be linear narratives, perhaps interrupted occasionally by clearly defined flashbacks.
>
> Style should be consistent.
>
> Unity of theme is essential.
>
> Tension and immediacy should be felt from the first.
>
> A single point of view generally works best, or a single defined narrator.
>
> Keep to a few characters, a few locales, and a limited time frame.
>
> Create a coherent shape that gives the story direction.

Some of these axioms seem as old as the idea of storytelling. Others may have come about with the development of the novel and the short story as artistic forms. Several may have resulted from contemporary notions of taste. But how do you know which is which? By experimenting with these boundaries you make breakthroughs, win freedoms, and understand the techniques of storytelling more fully. Our literature is continually being enriched by innovations and rediscoveries about style, subject, and the treatment of time, space, and human consciousness.

Some writers and artists have gone even farther. They've left narrative behind to reconceive literature not in terms of stories and novels but more as objects to be hung on museum walls. They've assaulted the mechanical conventions of the physical story itself. Why is everything in one typeface? Why are margins all the same? Why aren't there graphics? Can't pictures be part of it? Can literature be created as a unique object rather than as a reproducible form?

Ways in which people have responded to these inquiries have included a story in which each sheet was pasted on cardboard, little Christmas lights were pushed through the cardboard, and the instructions were to plug the story in before reading it. Another touching piece was a series of sad bar vignettes, written in smeary ballpoint pen on a packet of cocktail napkins.

Experiments, by their nature, are far more likely to fail than to succeed. And you can easily be seduced by your own ingenuity or get lost in the playground of self-indulgence. But what you find out in exploding the conventions might open up your fiction in ways that are as interesting as they are unpredictable.

See *Avant-garde, Convention, Metafiction.*

PART II

A CAUTIONARY
INTERLUDE

▼

WRITE WHAT YOU KNOW

◯ Some writers tell you, "Write what you know!"
Others tell you that half the great literature of the world would
be lost if people wrote only "what they knew." So it's important to figure out what *write what you know* can mean.

Taken most narrowly, it would mean write only about what
you have actually experienced. That does sound a bit limiting. Many writers are fundamentally—sometimes embarrass-
ingly—autobiographical. That might work for them, but it
doesn't seem appropriate as a general rule for all fiction.

A broader application of *write what you know* recognizes
that the idea of *you* is complex in itself. You, in theory at
least, know yourself. But your self is made up of many selves—

the girl who wanted an older brother, the high school misfit, the college student who dressed in black and wanted to join the French club, the woman who fantasizes about what she'd do with her own television talk show. You are, in part, not only persons you once were, but also persons you have tried to be, persons you have avoided being, and persons you fear you might be. All these are people you know.

A still broader notion of *write what you know* would recognize that you *know* in many ways. In fiction you can be your younger sister, your college roommate, your nervous boss, or your unhappy neighbor. Fiction based not on your own experience, but on experience you've observed is also writing about what you know. You know by empathy. You know by living.

So what kind of advice is *write what you know* anyway?

First, it's helpful to state the principle in reverse. "Don't write what you *don't* know." If you know nothing about Zaire, the federal penitentiary system, schizophrenia, or the French Revolution, you're unlikely to write about these things successfully. But then the situation gets more complicated.

We do have to acknowledge research as a legitimate way of knowing, or much fiction would be impossible. Writers immerse themselves in books on medical remedies, legal procedures, and haberdashery history for background information. They talk to plumbers, police officers, and podiatrists to gather authentic details.

We have to recognize imagination as a form of knowledge or our speculative fiction would vanish. Writers invent people they've never met, events that never happened, and countries that never existed.

But if your fiction is to live, something deeply immediate

and personal must be at its heart. Mark Twain made up stories, but he knew his Mississippi River, its people and its dialects. Hawthorne wrote about events that happened long before he was born, but he knew New England and its customs. Melville's fantastic voyages, although drenched in literary and encyclopedic sources, were launched from his own knowledge of the sea. Virginia Woolf created a character who lived for four centuries, but that character was inspired by a person she loved. Orwell invented a world of the future but it was based on his deep understanding of his own society.

Henry James got involved in this write-what-you-know argument when, in *The Art of Fiction,* he told a story of an Englishwoman who wrote a novel about French Protestant youth. She was praised for the portrait and was asked how she came by her experience. It came from a single glance at a group of young people but the woman knew what it was to be French, she knew about Protestantism, and she knew about being young, so she could imagine the characters in her novel.

Rather than giving us license to write about what we don't know, Henry James wants us to understand that the notion of experience is complicated. "The power to guess the unseen from the seen, to trace the implication of things, to judge the whole piece by the pattern, the condition of feeling life in general so completely that you are well on your way to knowing any particular corner of it—this cluster of gifts may almost be said to constitute experience." James astutely shifts the focus from the quantity of experience to the quality of experience by urging the writer, "Try to be one of the people on whom nothing is lost!"

That phrase deserves particular reflection. It recognizes that for writers experience is ultimately internal. A person may have worked on the railroad for forty years, traveled to exotic countries, or had a galaxy of escapades, but if that person is not observant, perceptive, and thoughtful about those experiences, that will show itself in the writing. On the other hand, if you have paid close attention, ideas for fiction will occur within the smallest compass. Educating yourself to be one of the people on whom nothing is lost is the deepest experience of all.

Think of Stephen Crane's *The Red Badge of Courage,* a Civil War classic written by a man who had not been on the battlefield. This novel has been justification for an infinite amount of "non-experienced" fiction. But *Red Badge* is not only a war story, it's a classic of psychological realism, of insight into men under stress, of a young man's fear, confusion, and self-delusion. Crane was writing about what he knew.

So *write what you know* is good advice, but should not be interpreted narrowly. There's a plenitude of possibility in what you know, what you can know, what you might want to know, and what it means to know.

▼

DON'T DO THIS:
A SHORT GUIDE
TO WHAT NOT TO DO

○○ *Don't try to tell too many stories at once.* ○○

Some writers, full of ideas and excitement, try to do too much in a single story, have too many incidents, too many plots. They want to tell about little Ilena, lost in the supermarket, but also about her mother, who is crying because she was arrested for shoplifting, and also about the dad, who's a manic-depressive who disappears for days but then shows up with beautiful toys, and about the new neighbors next door, who scream at each other all night—and the reader is soon as confused as little Ilena.

A story that's too complicated uses up its energy just to explain what's happening. Complication is not complexity.

A story that renders a single moment convincingly is a complex accomplishment. The complexity lies in the richness, the rendering, the texture, the subtlety of observation, the experience created for readers.

A beautifully complex story is often complex not because of a complicated surface but because of an impressive depth. See *Premise.*

∘∘ *Don't write stories in which the last lines are:* ∘∘

And then I woke up.

And then the alarm rang.

Well, they're bringing my supper now, steak and french fries they promised me. I guess they'll shave my head later, when the padre comes.

He realized he was alone, and slowly blinked his third eye.

It's not a bad place to live—warm, dry, and nice padded walls.

The guillotine blade fell swiftly, severing my head from my body.

"Doris, I'm gay."

He slowly drew the thin razor across his wrists.

He slowly shook out the whole bottle of pills in his hand.

He slowly put the muzzle of the gun against his forehead.

He slowly kept walking deeper into the water. He did not look back.

He pulled the sheet of paper out of the typewriter. The story was done.

What's wrong with these terrific last lines? They're all based on the same principle—surprise the reader. But who wants to read a whole story just for a punch line, especially ones that are this old?
See *Endings*.

∘∘ *Don't write about things* ∘∘
you don't know about.

Some beginnings make readers instantly suspicious.

"Mush, mush," Nooknook shouted, as he threw bits of meat to make his dogs bound across the ice floe.

Chichen Itza was especially beautiful on coronation day, thought Uxmalki as he carved on his chacmool.

If you don't know much about huskies or Mayans, basing your fiction on them will probably lead to trouble.
See *Accuracy*.

∘∘ *Don't write a story whose main point* ∘∘
is that it is from some unexpected point of view.

Such stories often end this way:

I can't help it if that's all I understand. After all, I'm just a dachshund.

(Or "just a parakeet," "just a teddy bear," etc.)

I've seen stories from the point of view of raccoons, roaches, deer, chairs, and, once, a pet rock. Writers have, of course, written fine stories from various points of view—animate and inanimate, human and nonhuman—but that's just their starting premise. The question is what is achieved by the device. An odd point of view may seem too cute, too contrived. It can seem to be nothing but a joke on the reader: you never guessed it was all being told by an eggbeater! Or it could be too sentimental and didactic (stories told by dog hit-and-run victims, foxes in traps, and caged chickens).

See *Point of View.*

∘∘ *Don't write stories* ∘∘
that are simply idea-driven.

When you have an idea—"Abortions are bad," "Alcoholism destroys homes," "Old people are neglected"—and you write a story mainly to exemplify that idea, you're giving your readers an *exemplum,* a little sermon that preaches by example. In a good story, however, the experience is primary, not a message. If you think of a story you admire, and someone asks you what its point is, you're likely to answer, "Well, it's about a lot of things." In other words, you felt that the story wasn't reducible to a single idea—it probably raised more questions than it answered.

See *Didacticism.*

∘∘ *Don't let your stories* ∘∘
have population explosions.

Readers lose track if there are too many names to retain. You must determine who is necessary to the story and remove everyone else from the set, forcibly if necessary.

> Arlo swung his mallet at Arlene's ball while Uncle Claude looked on admiringly. Arlo had a nice swing for a young man. Wilson was too easily distracted, and Roger was hopeless. If anything, Roger should really be paying attention to Arlene, not standing by the wicket snickering with Frederick and Carl about Benita falling off her big sorrel, Elena.

By this time, readers are looking for their own croquet mallets.

See *Character*.

> oo *Don't give your characters names* oo
> *that are phonetically similar unless you are*
> *deliberately trying to make a point.*

Characters with names like Jack and Kirk, Winston and Kingston, tend to run together in readers' minds. Jim and Susquehanna don't. Two-syllable names with diminutive endings have the same confusing effect: Vicky and Teddy and Cindy and Danny blur phonetically.

> oo *Don't preface your story with explanatory* oo
> *material that makes your readers impatient*
> *for the story to begin.*

Don't be like the guy who starts telling you an anecdote:

> This girl, I met her last Thursday, no it was Wednesday . . . wait, it *was* Thursday. I remember because I was getting

the laundry. Well really I was coming back with the laundry, and I had to stop for gas. My car doesn't hold but ten gallons, but I usually only buy two dollars at a time anyway. So I stopped at this little self-service place because I always pump my own—I mean I'm not a mechanic but I can pump my own gas. . .

Don't paint elaborate stage sets, don't have long overtures, don't have lengthy preambles, don't do formal introductions, don't keep readers wondering What is this about? When is this thing going to begin?

Good stories intrigue readers from the first words of the first sentence.

See *Beginnings, Exposition.*

oo *Don't write the following stories:* oo

THE BANGING-SHUTTER STORY: This is a story based on anticlimax. A perceived threat is built up by describing mysterious and frightening noises, sights, and sensations. The character's terror is developed by describing various fears and possibilities, and perhaps recent atrocities in the vicinity. The end reveals that it was all caused by a cat, a raccoon, a possum, a shutter, a loud clock, wind in the trees, moonlight in the mirror, a child's wind-up toy, one's own heartbeat. (Also known as the *I am der viper, I am der vindow viper story.*)

THE BATHTUB STORY: In the bathtub story a character stays in a single, relatively confined space for the whole story. While in that space the character thinks, remembers, worries, plans, whatever. Before long, readers realize that the character is not going to do anything. Nothing is going to happen in terms of action. The character is not interacting with other people, but is just thinking about past interactions. Problems will not be faced but thought about. Troubles will not occur but will be remembered. That's the problem with the bathtub story: The character is never going to get out of the bathtub.

Can a good bathtub story be written? Are there good bathtub stories? Of course, especially if the claustrophobia and lack of movement are exploited for suspense and tension. Bernard Malamud's *The Fixer* never gets out of prison. Samuel Beckett's character in *Malone Dies* never gets out of bed. But often the lack of motion signifies a failure of imagination. You must find a way to make up for the lack of plot, of action, and of momentum. The missing kinetic energy must be generated by particular daring, wit, or ingenuity. And even then, someone might say, "It's funny all right, but it's really just a bathtub story."

THE HOBOS-IN-SPACE STORY: Here a small number of characters, perhaps only two, isolated from ordinary society, talk a lot about life while not doing very much. They tend to comment about civilization, philosophize about meanings, and squabble a bit among themselves. One of them says, "It's cold." Another answers, "It's always been cold."

Perhaps this is all Samuel Beckett's fault. But it's really not fair to blame him. It *is* fair to blame those who don't realize that giving portentous dialogue to philosophizing outcasts (in a world gone mad) is self-indulgent, sentimental, and heavy-handed. The stylized setting makes all actions seem weightily symbolic, and the characters generally seem to stand for some major idea about the nature of man. Stories of this sort tend to end with either a bang (punching, knifing, hitting with a plank) or a whimper (staring into embers, staring into an empty pot, staring into nothing).

THE I-CAN-HARDLY-WAIT STORY: An I-can-hardly-wait sets up a character who will have his expectations dashed. A grandfather is depicted joyfully anticipating the arrival of a granddaughter. A woman is preparing an elaborate meal for the man of her dreams. A man is looking forward to his evening with the long-sought perfect woman. A child is waiting for her daddy to come home. The I-can-hardly-wait dwells on the joys expected and then deprives the central character of whatever is desired. The beloved one—man, woman, child, dog, or cat—inexplicably never shows up or is killed on the road or drunkenly calls from a bar or runs away with someone else or has really been dead for years.

It's true that life can be cruel, but this sort of story trivializes sad occurrences by focusing on the simple plot device of disappointed expectations. It's an easy way to manipulate readers, but it's too familiar a formula. Unless it brings readers to an insight beyond "Gee, you never know, do you? That was so sad," you haven't really created a story.

A variant of this is the *I-knew-the-last-line-when-I-read-the-first-line story.* That starts with the banker in a hurry knocking the bag lady into the gutter, the bully humiliating the defective child, the selfish man killing the good collie's half-breed puppies—pain is inflicted on some apparently helpless victim. Then we wait for the inevitable end. The bag lady has a secret mortgage and forecloses on the banker, the defective child ignores the screams of the bully imploring him to push the STOP button and lets the garbage compactor have its way with his tormentor, and the collie eats its owner in a lightning storm.

THE I-CRIED-BECAUSE-I-HAD-NO-SHOES-TILL-I-MET-A-MAN-WHO-HAD-NO-FEET STORY: This story is primarily designed to teach a lesson. Writers tell these to impart a moral, rather than to create an experience.

In these stories, characters do not have the idiosyncrasies of individuals. They have stereotyped traits—we have the unloving grandfather, the careless mother, or the ungrateful young girl. Events are set up to show the harmful consequences of bad behavior (or the beneficial results of good behavior), and the plot seems mechanical. If the effect of the ending is that this is the moral, this is the bottom line, the work will seem only like a lesson, a sermon, a homily.

Fine stories are written about characters learning, coming to understand, and having insights, but the I-cried-because story doesn't care about rendering psychological and emotional complexity. Instead, it tries to tell readers how to behave.

THE-LAST-LINE-SHOULD-BE-THE-FIRST-LINE STORY: There's a story that keeps getting told, a kind of urban legend, about a shy little guy who falls in love with a mysterious, lovely woman. They plan to get married, and the man's office friends throw a bachelor party, get him drunk, take him to a brothel, push him into a room, where he finds . . . guess who?

Now the question is, where should this story begin? It's just a long lead-up to a nasty surprise ending. It could be interesting if its ending was its beginning. How would two people behave in such a situation? Stories that lead up to revelations and odd situations really quit just where they should begin. An arrest, a compromising position, or a shocking discovery about a loved one will likely make a better opening than a closing. As an opening, there is high tension, interest, and momentum—readers want to know what happened next. As a conclusion, the revelation doesn't deal with the issue it raises.

THE WEIRD HAROLD STORY: Weird Harolds are stories focused on a character who is strange and different. Readers are given many examples of the character's behavior, but no insight into the character. Writers of Weird Harold stories are fascinated with a character who certainly seems worthy of fictional representation. However, they haven't figured out a shape that gives readers what they need in order to know the character from the inside, what might be driving him, what he might be searching for, what might be missing that makes him do what he does.

This does not mean you should go in for overt psychologizing, or provide a secret reason to explain complex behavior. But there has to be a sense of how the character perceives and thinks. If you can embed information in an evocative anecdote—include the story about the time the character's older brothers stuffed him into a laundry bag and left him on the sidewalk—we can begin to feel the character's emotional processes, see the world through his eyes. We may not fully understand what's going on, but we don't expect a character to be fully explained. If a character is wholly inexplicable, though, readers can only say, "That's weird," or "That's really strange." And that doesn't make a story. (Or it does—a Weird Harold.)

THE ZERO-TO-ZERO STORY: If the beginning of a story presents a character who appears rigid and dull and the story simply demonstrates that the character is rigid and dull, readers and the story haven't gone anywhere. Zero-to-zero lends itself to heavy-handed ironies: the story of the loser who tries but loses once more; the chronic cheater who, when presented with a moral choice, cheats again; the alcoholic who goes back to the bottle; the suicide who finally succeeds. These stories also tend to dwell on one characteristic, usually a weakness or a vice.

This type of story just acts out what readers learned right at the beginning. A variant teases readers with the possibility that there is more to the person than is first presented, but the story returns to zero with an ending that corroborates the beginning. Readers still haven't been taken anywhere. The longer the story, the further they haven't gone.

THE ZERO-TO-ONE-HUNDRED STORY: In this story, a character totally overcomes some character problem. But a major, permanent change in personality is difficult to make plausible in a short story.

Behavior lies deep and is rooted in habits and responses that cannot simply vanish in a wish or a phrase. The way a person has behaved or the way people have behaved toward a person affects everyone for a long time, whether they like it or not. You cannot eradicate the past merely by saying so. To write otherwise is to be simplistic.

Massive character change is a staple of commercial entertainment. Half-hour situation comedies or one-hour mystery shows rely over and over again on a formula in which various family members finally realize they love each other or have behaved badly, but now everything is all right. These endings are emotionally attractive but, deep down, we know they just aren't true.

○○ *Don't believe any of the don'ts above.* ○○

Art is made out of broken rules. Art pushes at the envelope of the never-done, but also constantly recycles the forever-done. Clichés are the compost of art. Transformations, inversions, reversions, and conversions continually revive fiction. If you dare, these don'ts can be your pleasure ground.

PART III

FROM ACCURACY TO ZIGZAG: AN ALPHABET FOR WRITERS OF FICTION

▼

ACCURACY
:
○ Accuracy refers to how well writers have observed the world. It means showing respect for the most minute details and the deepest truths of your subjects. If readers feel that the observations are genuine, then the fictional world comes alive.

For example, a little girl watches every step as her grandmother simmers prunes in ginger wine for a Stockholm pudding. Readers believe in the scene because they believe in the pudding. How could you make up Stockholm pudding? Accurately rendered actions, objects, and talk actualize the world and create characters.

Accuracy doesn't mean that the fiction has to be realistic

in the conventional sense. If you're creating an imaginary world, your accuracy depends on the story's building logically and faithfully according to its own premises. Joseph Heller's *Catch-22* is weirdly accurate. The war was real, the number of bombing missions was continually increased, pilots did get their morphine stolen from their first-aid kits, a black market existed, men did go crazy. Heller based his surreal world on that actuality.

A lack of accuracy makes readers think that writers don't know what they are talking about. A passementerie importer complains about the decline of European workmanship: "I can get better from Singapore." That does sound like something you'd hear in a New York luncheonette, and you believe in the story. But if the writer has his character get out of the subway "and stroll down Main Street," readers think, This writer doesn't know New York, and they don't believe in the fictional world.

There is a moral as well as aesthetic imperative to be accurate. If you depict a Maori, for example, I think you're obligated to have some real understanding of the world of the Maori. If you make up ceremonies and customs, you're exploiting the naïveté or preconceptions of your audience. Serious writers do serious research when they need to. Don't think, This is fiction—I don't have to check my facts. Even minor errors can make your readers doubt you. You want your readers to feel: I don't think this is made up; this sounds as though it really happened.

See *Local Color, Realism,* "Write What You Know."

▼
ADVICE

o   Naturally you want other people to read your
work, but advice from others on your writing is a tricky business. Loved ones, friends, and acquaintances are often not
reliable critics. Their love for you can make them think anything you do is wonderful because you did it. Even though
you have begged them to be honest, they feel awkward criti-
cizing your work. Another problem is more complicated.
People close to you may want to believe you're a certain type
of person. When your fiction violates that image, they feel
uncomfortable and tend not to like those aspects of your work.
Just because your friends have the good taste to like you does
not mean that they can recognize or assess the strengths and
weaknesses of your writing.

There's another problem too. You must deal with what
friends say. What if someone you love tells you that you can't
write and should give it up? Should you give up writing? Give
up your friend? Get depressed? What if someone you love
gives you advice that doesn't seem right? Should you follow
it because there will be hurt feelings if you don't?

The advice you need for revision should come from people
whose taste in fiction (not in music, art, or life-style) you
respect. Encouragement is important. Some writers and critics use their formidable knowledge and sophisticated taste in
literature as a stick to beat on others. Though such people
can be perceptive, it seems as if they want to squelch all voices
but their own. The people who can help you are those who
are sympathetic to the kind of work you're doing, knowledgeable about it, and supportive in their criticism.

See *Reading, Revision, Workshops.*

▼

ALLEGORY

In allegory, characters and even places can represent historical forces, philosophical ideas, or spiritual values. The plot dramatizes the conflict among those abstractions. The great example in English fiction is John Bunyan's *Pilgrim's Progress* in which a character named Christian (the man struggling to be religious and good) travels toward the Celestial City (Heaven) while having to pass by such perils as the Slough of Despond, Vanity Fair, and Doubting Castle (the sins of despair, pride, and skepticism). Probably the best-known modern allegory is George Orwell's satirical *Animal Farm* in which the revolt of the farm animals represents the Russian Revolution in particular and revolutions in general.

Writing lively allegorical fiction demands giving the characters their own vitality, their own individuality, so that they are not simply talking ideas or disguised moral principles.

However, there always seems to be an allegorical undertone in fiction, with characters embodying some problem like Blinded by Ambition, Incapable of Giving Love, or Too Stupid to Get Hurt. They, too, have to be believable people first. Humor can make allegory palatable. The beasts in fables are often allegorical, standing for such things as Foolish Pride or Miserliness.

But fiction has to succeed on its own terms. Ideas don't bring life to a story. The story brings life to the ideas.

See *Parable, Symbolism.*

▼

ALLUSION

○ You can enliven and enrich your narrative with the names of real people, ideas, objects, and creations. Allusions to *Key Largo* or *The Picture of Dorian Gray* help establish a character's taste and the time of the fiction, and embed certain ideas and themes. Some writers allude heavily, using popular music or even advertising jingles to create a feeling of immediacy and authenticity. Thomas Pynchon's World War II novel, *Gravity's Rainbow,* is filled with thousands of well-known and obscure popular culture references from *Flit* to Primo Scala's Accordion Band. Other writers avoid ephemeral allusions, perhaps to deemphasize the specific historical event the fiction is based on, as in Norman Mailer's World War II novel, *The Naked and the Dead.*

Keep in mind that allusions only work for readers who recognize the allusion. References to Niobe or the Heisenberg principle depend on knowledgeable readers. If you say a character's favorite song is Muddy Waters' "Got My Mojo Working," you create no impression on those who don't know its raunchy lyrics.

Instead of risking an allusion whose point might be totally lost, embed description so that readers can have a sense of its significance.

> Hill put on his Roscoe Holcomb album and lay down in the darkness. The high mountain voice was full of a pain so keen and lonesome that, as Hill's eyes filled with tears, he felt strangely comforted.

Readers who have never heard of Roscoe Holcomb can still imagine the music.

Opinions differ about allusions to brand names like Benetton, Yugos, or "Where's the beef?" commercials. Some writers feel that such references capture the real texture of the time. Others feel that they are a cheap grab at a false authenticity—the fiction will be outdated as quickly as the faddish names. But if you choose well and your characters speak of the books and music that really are the essence of their existence, you can capture that moment for later generations, as F. Scott Fitzgerald did in *The Great Gatsby*.

Allusions can range from references you would expect virtually all your readers to recognize, such as "He was a Mack truck body run by a Moped brain," to others that might be pretty obscure (Woody Allen has a joke that depends on knowing the name of the president of the New York City Teachers Union). Self-indulgence is one of the great sins of writing, but some esoteric allusions can simultaneously delight your best audience and express your own more private world.

See *Character, Narrator, Style, Texture.*

▼

AMBIGUITY

The difference between ambiguity and confusion can be puzzling to beginning writers. Ambiguity is the controlled and deliberate presentation of a limited number of possible interpretations. For example, the central concern of fiction by Nathaniel Hawthorne or Henry James is often an unfathomable mystery. In James's *The Turn of the Screw,* the central question is whether the governess is to be trusted. Does she see real ghosts? Is she hallucinating? Is she lying for some reason? Are the children plotting against her? Is she completely mad? Any one answer would seem an oversimplification. And that's the point. James leaves it ambiguous because ambiguity is what the story is about. In *The Scarlet Letter,* Hawthorne is ambiguous about which character is truly immoral. Again, the ambiguity is the point.

Confusion, on the other hand, is the lack of control that results when you omit or leave blurry certain information your readers need to know. Sometimes writers get defensive about what they left out. Every time a reader says, "This seems unclear. I couldn't figure out what was going on in this scene. Were they in the house or in the field? How old were these characters? Was that a man or a woman? What *did* happen in the end?" the writer says, "Yeah, that's the way I meant it. To be subtle. You know. I didn't want to make everything obvious." It is as if the writer wants the reader to make up for his own vagueness and lack of energy.

Be crisply definitive. John Updike's encyclopedic precision suggests more profound mysteries. Significant ambiguities rise not from withholding information but from being richly informative.

See *Negative Positive Knowledge.*

▼

ANTI-HERO

○ This term usually refers to an unconventional central character who lacks the virtues of the traditional hero, but for whom we are to feel sympathy nonetheless.

Rogues, fools, and dreamers have made lively central characters and anti-heroes for hundreds of years. Cervantes' Don Quixote attacks windmills. Sterne's Tristram Shandy goes around in circles. Defoe's Moll Flanders inverts conventional morality. Dostoyevsky's Underground Man and Kafka's Joseph

K. unsuccessfully confront the bureaucratic mechanisms and philosophical afflictions of modern life. Joseph Heller's Yossarian makes cowardice a form of virtue.

But a jerk is no anti-hero. If you want to write about boors and bigots, winos and whiners, you have to figure out a way to make these characters interesting and not merely incompetent or repulsive. If you don't, your readers won't care whether your character gets his art in the gallery or gets kicked out on the street, won't particularly want him to get the woman he claims he longs for, and might even be disappointed that she seems blind to his cretinism.

For an anti-hero to work as a protagonist, he needs saving graces. He might be a boozer, a brawler, or an irresponsible louse, but readers have to be convinced that he has some real talents or virtues. You want the reader to have some emotional investment in him. That takes some strategy. Just because the character tells us what a great and unjustly misunderstood person he is doesn't mean we will believe it. The opposite might be true. Characters in love with themselves do not come across as the most reliable of witnesses.

If you make your character witty, or perceptive, or peculiarly thoughtful, readers realize that he may behave erratically but something worthwhile is underneath. If you let readers understand the circumstances that created his personality, so that his vices or crimes are understood as reactions to things that were done to him, sympathy results. That doesn't mean readers will approve of his acts, but it does mean that they may care what happens to him, hope he mends his ways, are saddened by his setbacks, and feel that the experience of knowing him through fiction has been worthwhile. In Wright's tragic novel, *Native Son,* the main character keeps doing things that make readers think, Oh no. Don't do that. But Wright provides an understanding that keeps readers emotionally engaged even as they are shocked.

Anti-heroes can be unwilling victims, wise fools, and innocent misfits who have been ostracized by their cultures and whose powerlessness gives them anti-hero status. They are comic saints and baggy-pantsed martyrs witnessing the corruptness of the world. Kingsley Amis's *Lucky Jim* flops through the world of academia. In Thomas Pynchon's *Gravity's Rainbow,* Tyrone Slothrop is whirled through post–World War II chaos, losing his directions, his bearings, even his name. The unlikely hero of John Kennedy Toole's *A Confederacy of Dunces* is a hopeless anachronism. Through them you can see how vulnerability, sensitivity, or idealism can lurk inside problematic protagonists.

Anti-heroes afflicted with passivity are a problem. Victims can be main characters, but if they are passive, always acted upon rather than acting, they get tiresome. Readers tend to be first irritated and then bored by someone who just lets things happen to him time after time. The very narrative seems to lose energy, and a sudden upturn at the end can't save it. The worm must be trying to turn, even if it can only writhe.

The person you love to hate is another category of anti-hero. This is not merely a cad or a clod, but a character who is so energetically awful that you're fascinated by his evil schemes—villains like Satan in *Paradise Lost* who are heroic in their villainy. Readers can become fascinated by malevolence, especially if they feel the character is his own worst enemy and, though he brings pain to others, he somehow always loses. Writers have often been disconcerted to find their cruel characters more memorable than their theoretically admirable heroes and heroines.

The old-fashioned hero and heroine aren't really taken seriously anymore as characters—our notions of psychology and human behavior seem too sophisticated for such simplicity. So even your admirable characters will have some negative traits. You can use these flaws not only to make your characters more realistic, but also to make them more interesting, more complex, and, oddly, even more likable.

See *Character, Hero, Picaro.*

▼

ARCHETYPE

An archetype suggests mythical divinities, ancient forces, and primal experiences. A father in a story might be a patriarchal archetype reminding readers of the notion of fatherhood, kingship, Zeus, or God the Father. A mother may intimate motherhood, the idea of nurturing, or Mother Earth.

Birth, coming of age, dying—the rhythms of day and night, summer and winter—are archetypal events. Carl Jung, the Swiss psychologist, said that all people, regardless of their culture, hold these experiences in their *collective unconscious* and naturally gravitate to stories that reflect human history through archetypal symbols.

Some writers try to create figures that are archetypes before they are characters. These usually don't come to life on the page. Sometimes writers leave these effigies unnamed since they fear that specificity might diminish them as archetypes.

These ponderous creations, appelated something like "The Mother" or "The Artist," often seem carved out of stone.

Great writers have understood that if you create a fresh, individual character or a vivid, moving experience you suggest all human experience—all that has gone before and that is yet to come. The more specific and individuated a character is—like Flaubert's Emma Bovary or Joyce's Stephen Dedalus or Twain's Huck Finn—the more universal and archetypal the character can be. If you're afraid that specificity of detail limits the significance of your characters, you'll cut yourself off from your most original and vital material.

See *Myth, Objective Correlative, Stereotype, Symbolism.*

▼

ATMOSPHERE

○ To establish a particular atmosphere, mood, or tone, you must pay attention to your readers' short memory for sensation. If the atmosphere is to be foreboding, you must forebode on every page. If it is to be cold, you must chill, not once or twice, but until your readers are shivering. Remember that you're creating an experience, not just imparting data. Sensory information once said is not enough said. Our own experience tells us that a hangover is a constant presence for its full duration no matter what else we are doing. Don't be afraid of repetition.

Atmosphere isn't just weather. It is setting—stuffed furniture, dark carpets, and thick velvet throws can suggest claustrophobia, just as Formica and aluminum can give a sense of sterility. Landscapes can connote death or life, foreboding or hope. Sounds, sights, and smells all are part of atmosphere. Toni Morrison's *Song of Solomon* is an anthology of atmosphere—one house is choked with death, another vibrant with life; her landscapes range from threatening to liberating. These atmospheric details are ways of enriching the texture of a story, of bringing in sensory detail, of creating the fullness of experience, of making the reader be there.

See *Description*.

▼

AVANT-GARDE

o Although artists over the centuries have extended the possibilities of literature in many ways, the term *avant-garde* is generally used for those spirited modernists who consciously assaulted traditional notions of art. In literature Gertrude Stein, Ezra Pound, James Joyce, and Samuel Beckett inverted the rules they inherited, and profoundly influenced all who followed them.

Since avant-garde writers challenge readers' preconceptions and expectations, they are, almost by definition, difficult. They often do not seem concerned with grace or beauty or readability. Gertrude Stein wrote about innovation, "As Pablo once remarked, when you make a thing, it is so complicated making it that it is bound to be ugly, but those that do it after you they don't have to worry about making it and they can make it pretty, and so everybody can like it when the others make it." Gertrude Stein is an example herself. Most readers find her repetitive and obscure, but her discoveries about language and style were incorporated by writers like Sherwood Anderson and Ernest Hemingway.

Contemporary writers continue to discover new frontiers, new ways of challenging themselves, their readers, and the critics. Their experiments continually critique our ideas about what art is. But there is a price. Most avant-garde writers have only a small, fairly sophisticated readership. Even if their books are praised by prestigious critics, writers like Walter Abish tend to have limited sales, and they must find adventurous, independent presses to publish their work. Others, like Gilbert Sorrentino or Renata Adler, have developed larger audiences.

See *Convention, Explosion, Metafiction, Tour de Force.*

▼

BATHOS

○ This is a negative term used when writers have tried so hard to make their readers cry—loading misery on sadness—that their work seems contrived, silly, and unintentionally funny. Soap opera has that effect when you read a synopsis of all the complexities that beset people in a single episode:

> Robert is suffering from an hereditary liver disease. His wife Emilia has been arrested for cocaine smuggling. Their amnesiac son has disappeared again, and their house has mysteriously burned to the ground. Robert learns that his business enemies are plotting to kidnap Margo, his mistress. As he is driving to stop them, Robert runs over his beloved cat.

A convincing plot develops out of the original situation you present. If you keep adding new problems that have nothing to do with the original situation, readers start disbelieving. For example, a story about a violent alcoholic who is having trouble with his marriage has certain natural possibilities, but if in the middle of the story his brother gets arrested for

smuggling diamonds, his mother starts being blackmailed by
an old lover, and his daughter gets leukemia, readers will feel
the story is adventure, fantasy, or farce.

However, life can be bathetic, a chaotic mess of unbelievable miseries that leaves the sufferer unable to respond nor-
mally. If you're determined to tell such a story, a strategy that
forestalls criticism is to state up front that a number of catas-
trophes occurred within a short space of time. In other words,
build the problems into the premise of the story. By the end
of the first chapter of Bernard Malamud's *The Assistant* you
have felt his characters' economic misery, personal unhappi-
ness, domestic tension, and moral angst—you aren't surprised that those circumstances all play a part. A successful
novel, with all its twists and turns, ups and downs, is based
on a relatively clear set of premises.

Bathos is a failure of form rather than of content. It occurs
when writers haven't thought of the shape that is needed to
support the world they want to create.

See *Cliché, Melodrama, Sentimentality.*

▼

BEGINNINGS

o   The advice in *Alice in Wonderland* is, in its
own way, unimpeachable: "Begin at the beginning, go on to
the end. Then stop." But in fiction that's not as simple as it
first appears. Where the beginning is, what it is, and how to
do it constantly troubles writers.

In the first draft of a story, no rules apply. You write and
write, ideas come, characters change, situations grow, dia-
logues take off, speeches become scenes, and surprises occur.
You aren't deciding where the story begins, where it ends,

and where it will stop. It is not there yet. It is being created; it is creating itself. It's hard to know what's happening, and it might be best not to think about it too much anyway. The less critical judgment you have at this point—the less you let taste, inhibition, second-guessing, and anxiety get in the way—the better off you're likely to be.

After this draft exists, then you can bring to bear some of your critical faculties and see what you can see about your creation. Then you can try to discover what story you have made, which is not necessarily the story you started out to make. You might find, for example, that you have started telling one story, then another, and then still another.

At this point you have to decide which story you want to tell this time. When you do, you will have a clearer sense of where this particular story should begin, as opposed to the other stories that are in your draft, which might be your stories of the future. The first several paragraphs or pages of a first draft may read like a warm-up. The story really kicks in on the third page. That beginning might simply be abandoned. Or a wonderful beginning no longer suits the story that you've decided to write. Nice as it is, it needs to go. Or you labor miserably over the beginning, believing you must get it right to go on with the story, when the reverse might be true. If you write the rest of the story, then you'll be able to write the beginning.

Remember, begin with tension and immediacy. Make readers feel the story has started. They want to be in your world, not be told about it. Don't preface—plunge in.

Begin does not necessarily mean starting with the first event in a string of events that leads chronologically to the last event. A story of a shoe salesman's nervous breakdown might have begun when he dropped out of college because he was home-sick. The finished story itself might begin with him crying while he is setting up a Thom McAn's "Shoes for the Whole Family" seasonal display.

In fact, short stories usually begin somewhere close to their endings. That doesn't violate the principle of beginning at the beginning, but instead serves to highlight an important distinction. Perhaps the shoe salesman's story really began before he was born. But this particular fiction, this piece of art, begins when he started to cry.

Beginnings are a tough business. They need to be intriguing and energetic. Readers and editors are impatient. They don't read far if their attention is not engaged by the opening page.

See *Coincidence, Endings, Exposition, Premise.*

▼

CATHARSIS

If you are determined to have a work end with loss, failure, death, abandonment, or other assorted miseries, you have to figure out a way to make your readers feel that their pain is worthwhile and rewarding. That's a serious challenge.

Catharsis, the term made famous by Aristotle in his discussion of tragedy, refers to the sensation of exaltation that can result from experiencing sadness and fear. But what happens and why are not perfectly clear. Catharsis literally means purging. It can make you feel both exhausted and elated, as if you were emotionally scoured. Catharsis can make an audience understand the inevitable sufferings of all humanity. And catharsis can be an intellectual moment that gives you a private recognition. Tragic endings can create a meaningful, beneficial, even exhilarating experience for an audience.

The question is how to make unhappy endings work. A classic strategy, as in *Romeo and Juliet,* is to make it clear from the beginning that your audience is viewing a tragedy. Readers are psychologically prepared from the start to focus on how plans go awry, the psychology of the characters, and the fickleness of fortune. (Even though we still hope, every time, that this time they will escape happily.) Another way is through close attention to foreshadowing, as in Gustave Flaubert's *Madame Bovary,* where a gradual darkening of the lives of the characters makes Emma's suicide not only inevitable and appropriate, but even a sort of release from pain.

At one time the "four-handkerchief" book or movie was very popular. Audiences looked forward to a good cry. Right now, people seem to be made uncomfortable by unhappy endings. They want things to come out right for the characters they like. The reasons for that are too complicated to talk about here. Perhaps in a secular society tragic endings are no longer seen as meaningful, perhaps contemporary audiences feel overburdened by the enormous tragedies of late-twentieth-century life. But as a writer you need to be aware that tragic endings are a problem. Your story has to transfigure the sadness you create so readers feel catharsis (whatever it may be), and not depression (they already know what that is too well).

Catharsis ultimately is an aesthetic term. It means you did it right. Your readers don't feel cheated or disappointed or manipulated by the tragic end. You created a world in which the pattern was fulfilled by the darkness that brought it to a close.

See *Endings, Poetic Justice, Resolution, Sentimentality.*

▼
CHARACTER

○ The creation of character presents special problems for writers of fiction. The playwright or screenwriter can hope for arresting actors whose appearance, presence, mannerisms, and delivery will help create memorable characters. As a writer you have only your words on the page. You cannot even rely on illustration, as nineteenth-century writers often did. At the same time, there's nothing more important to your fiction than your characters.

So with only the words on the page, what must you do to create character?

First you need to understand that your mind might visualize *Bella came into the living room,* but your readers know only that an unknown entity, presumably female, whose name is Bella, has been put in a certain situation. There is a predisposition to be interested in her because you have focused on her. Your readers await more information.

That information can come in many ways. You might tell your readers about Bella, as people tell about friends or relatives whose lives and histories they know well:

Bella was a handsome brunette in her mid-thirties. *Handsome* was the word people used, probably because men found her attractive but intimidating.

That information, as in real life, is selective and interpretive. After reading the description we are inclined to view Bella in a certain way.

Or you could describe what Bella does upon entering the living room. If she starts cleaning up imaginary lint from the sofa, one sort of person is suggested. If she spills her scotch and lets it sink into her skirt without seeming to care, that suggests another. Something prosaic like sitting down and reading the newspaper does not tell readers much. But if she turns at once to the medical column, that might tell us something. The actions you give your characters should be densely informative. If her actions are rendered vividly, we know Bella without entering her mind in great depth.

A character is also directly created by what she says. Simply calling a character boring or witty doesn't engage or convince readers. They aren't experiencing the character—they're just being told about her. But if readers hear the character speak, they can make up their own minds:

> Before we could drink, Bella insisted on explaining to us how champagne was made and how there are two methods, one was better than the other, but she didn't remember which, but that one involved rotating bottles and the other had something to do with vats. "The man at the store said you could tell the difference on the label, but he left before I figured out what part of the label it was. *Brut*—I think it means it was made by force. That sounded like the cheap way, so I got the ones marked *Sec* which has to mean delicate, right? You're not going to get me to drink champagne that comes out of vats. But the guy told me there really wasn't that much difference, they both got up your nose the same way."

Let your character talk not simply for plot or exposition, but to create the person for the reader. Then she starts to live. Talk alone can create a character and a story.

The most intimate way of knowing a character is through her mind, her ideas and memories, her fears and hopes. She may speak little and do less, but her thoughts can give readers the feeling that they understand her:

> Bella knew how she sounded, felt the words twisting away from her. There was some reason an old-fashioned way of doing something was better than a cheap way even if hardly anyone could tell the difference, but she could feel the idea getting confused and the panicky sense that not only had she gotten it wrong, but no one even cared if she did. "Oh hell," she said, "let's drink up."

Thoughts lead us to feel strongly for characters, to worry over them, so that even when they misbehave we feel sympathy for their inability to live up to their best selves. The more you let your readers know, the more they are likely to be interested in the tensions between thought and behavior.

An absent character can also be a powerful figure in a story. She'd be created by the effects she's had on others. The other characters seem to be under her influence—their conversation keeps returning to her, and their mosaic of impressions makes her present though she never appears. In novels, talk about a character is often used to pique our interest and to heighten the arrival of the character. But with such an extended fanfare, the character had better live up to the advance publicity.

Physical description is useful in making your readers see the character, not merely to describe what the character looks like in the ordinary sense of the information that appears on driver's licenses, but in order to give the character corporeal life. Flesh has heft, takes up space, feels through its skin. A fat thigh or a bony arm makes a person more vivid than height and eye color. A spectacularly running nose is worth a paragraph of prosaic physical description.

Minor characters are extraordinarily important. Goofs, worms, and slugs are vividly remembered. Creeps, twerps, and bruisers are filled with life. Neurasthenics and parvenus enrich the texture of narratives and become memorable figures in their own right. Since they tend to appear briefly, they must be established strongly and clearly, and they must be invested with traits that are both distinctive and recognizable.

Minor characters are often given a distinguishing feature, and every time they appear we are reminded of that peculiarity. If the trait is simple, like a character who hiccups whenever he appears, or says "Whoops, golly me" in every scene, the character is called *flat*. That isn't necessarily a negative term. It means that the character is functioning more like a prop than a person. If he has a few more features with some emotional resonance (maybe he's a vivid whiner), the character becomes *round,* or half-round perhaps. So a comic doorman who always drops luggage becomes a more developed figure if he shows a picture of his family who admire him a great deal because of his smart uniform and important responsibilities. E. M. Forster's classic *Aspects of the Novel* (1927) talks about this dimensional declension of characters from flat to round.

What happens to main characters is intimately involved with the definition of the short story. Some people feel a short story is a narrative that shows a change in a character. Without that change, the story is merely an incident or an anecdote.

Change usually means psychological change—realization, revelation, revision, epiphany, understanding, decision. Whether that is the only way of defining a story is open to question, but it does remain the ultimate criterion for significant numbers of writers, editors, critics, and ordinary readers.

See *Anti-hero, Archetype, Facade, Flashback, Hero, Juggling, Motif, Names, Position, Stereotype, Suspense.*

▼

CLICHÉ

A cliché is a literary feature that has been used so often that it has burned out and died.

Finding out what is a cliché and what is not is a matter of learning. Beginning writers think it's ingenious to write a story about someone trying to write a story. They are told that the idea is a cliché itself. Then they know. Recognizing clichéd expressions, images, characters, and plots is not in the genetic code. Sensitivity comes from reading and experience.

In matters of plot it's easy to get confused about what is a cliché. Certain stories will always be told—characters will fight tyrannical governments, fall in love, risk their lives for power, and go on first dates. They're clichés if there's nothing new in your treatment, and they're good fiction if your energy and insight give them life.

This goes for characters, too. There will always be characters that have been used over and over—neurotic parents, sensitive children, friendly bartenders. They're clichés if you just treat them as everyone else has, and they're alive if you draw them freshly.

Even single words can be clichés. All words are created

equal, but some words have grown more tired than others. That's true not only of adjectives like *unique* or *azure* but even of certain function words. *As,* for example. Over the years writers have used *as* to get more information into their sentences:

> "No," he said, as he leaned back in his red leather chair.

That use of *as* as a coordinating conjunction between two main clauses looks harmless and certainly is not toxic. But there's something so familiar in it that it reminds readers of commercial magazine stories. There can't be anything intrinsically wrong with *as* used in this way, but look for it in opening sentences of admired, anthologized stories, and you're not likely to find it. The same thing is true for *while:*

> "What's up with you?" asked Mary, while raising her can of Diet Coke.

Then there are words that are like literary fossils, not the richly evocative fossils of obsolete words, but those that have remained in writing because they have remained in writing. The verb *don,* for example:

> Mr. Garvish donned his gray raincoat, as he stared at us angrily.

I don't know if I've ever heard a human say *don* aloud in normal conversation. There can't be anything wrong with *don,* but it and words like it suggest that writers aren't paying close attention to the world or to their language.

Others come to mind: *blurt.* At one time characters frequently blurted. They often blurted sentences that were quite long—perhaps too long to be truly blurted. It is like the overuse of *gushed, chortled,* and *beamed.* These words seem to have a sinister life of their own.

Fiction writing is less susceptible than journalistic writing to another class of problematic words. These are vogue words that seem to spring into general use and then are heard everywhere. They come from the political bureaucracy, from science (popular psychology especially), and from news events. Soon all sorts of people are *assuming postures* or *networking* or *defining windows* or *undergoing devolution* or *getting in touch with their feelings* and so forth. This sort of language can be useful to a fiction writer. If you listen for trends in usage, you can suggest a great deal about a character or a social group through conversation. Then you have recognized the cliché, not succumbed to it. But you need take care— vogue words can date your story as fast as they disappear themselves.

The familiar phrases of conventional fiction signal to readers that the work is going to be as predictable as its prose. For some readers and writers that is a virtue. Jean Kent and Candace Shelton's *The Romance Writers' Phrase Book* is a perversely helpful book. Designed for romance writers, it is filled with suggested phrases like "the thought froze in her brain," "something clicked in her mind," and "she shuddered, bristling with indignation." It suggests descriptions such as "her hips tapered into long straight legs" and "his ruggedly handsome face was vaguely familiar." For romance readers, that language signals that the book is what they are looking for. But for other readers, those phrases can mean that the work is not going to be fresh, original, and thoughtful. In fact, *The Romance Writers' Phrase Book* might be a useful anti-dictionary for writers. Phrases of this sort often simplify reality. They do not describe what is seen but substitute a convention for the observation.

Clichés of perception combine familiar observations with familiar language: "He was a blond Adonis"; "She had a body that just wouldn't quit." "She slipped into her bikini" is a conventional phrase which, when you think about it, totally misrepresents that action for modern materials and most mortals. Here the writer is falling back on tired phrases and weak thoughts.

Some writers have collected the "countless hours" and "sighs of relief" they come upon. Frank Sullivan of *The New Yorker* would write little essays stringing together as many clichés as he could. The philologist Eric Partridge compiled *A Dictionary of Clichés* and wrote an essay in *A Charm of Words* mentioning that O. Henry wrote a story about a code that could only be deciphered if you knew enough clichés.

But clichés are not a laughing matter to aspiring serious writers. The editorial eye does not look upon them kindly and tends to dismiss writers who let hackneyed expressions and trite phrases infest their prose.

Blockbuster fiction, genre fiction, commercial fiction—whatever you call it—has different standards. There clichés seem to make little difference. Commercial fiction calls for high energy, momentum, excitement, movement, action. The familiar language of clichés makes the prose read more quickly and easily. Readers don't want to wrestle with words, but to move fast and furiously, passionately or fearfully. The familiar language does not undercut the sensations. It may even help to evoke them.

See *Diction*, "Don't Do This," *Formula, Genre, Pathetic Fallacy, Reading, Sentimentality, Stereotype, Style.*

▼

CLIFF-HANGER

o The differences between the cliff-hangers of Henry James and those of Zane Grey are not as great as you might suppose. Both writers know that predicaments, entanglements, difficulties, and dilemmas keep readers engaged. Zane Grey's cliffs might be stonier, but for his characters in their own world Henry James's are just as perilous.

Detective, horror, espionage, and Western fiction rely heavily on physical danger. Readers feast happily on narrow escapes, daring rescues, and close calls. Will he escape? How will he escape? Readers need to have these questions answered immediately: "I couldn't put it down," they say. "I stayed up all night reading it."

But in fiction about human relations, psychological predicaments create similar excitement. Should Madame Bovary accept an invitation from the seductive Rodolphe? Will she borrow even more money? Jane Austen's novels hang on the cliffs of love, marriage, loneliness, and happiness. Kafka's *The Trial* combines external and internal cliff-hangers. Will Joseph K. escape his guards? Did he just say the worst possible thing? Should he have gone into that dark cathedral? We have to keep reading to find out.

See *Plot, Position, Suspense, Tension.*

▼
COINCIDENCE

o A coincidence can make an intriguing premise. For example, a woman executive, happily married to a handsome airline pilot, goes to a business conference and meets, by chance, Dorcas, a red-headed girl she teased so cruelly throughout fourth grade that the girl transferred to another school.

Further coincidences, however, weaken plausibility. If it turns out that both women are competing for the same job, the story starts to sound contrived. Readers sense you're going to teach some moral lesson, or set up a clever twist. It's even more problematic if you resolve the story by another coincidence—the women talk together and realize they're both married to the same man! Your readers have been betrayed. You created a world they were willing to take seriously, but then you relied on a trick to end the story.

If coincidence is meant to play a part in your story you can forestall criticism by building the coincidence into the premise of the fiction. We are not surprised that two couples end up at the same resort if it is established early that the resort is where people of a certain class traditionally stay. If the town is small enough, we know their lives might have intertwined before. Carefully done, coincidences can seem more inevitable than contrived.

Deus ex machina is the Latin term for implausible coincidences and mechanical surprises that are invented by writers to make their plots come out a certain way, generally to satisfy the sentimental hopes of the audience. It's the bolt of lightning that causes the horse to rear up and toss the villain over the cliff, the flash flood that reveals the vein of gold to the loving couple.

In farce and comedy, though, outrageous coincidences and *deus ex machina* inventions are often part of the fun. Henry Fielding's *Tom Jones* is full of fortuitous rescues, unfortunate misunderstandings, and surprise meetings that both complicate and ultimately resolve the plot. Charles Dickens and other nineteenth-century writers used coincidence to bring novels to closure. In *Oliver Twist,* characters whom Oliver stumbles on by chance turn out to be related to him in significant ways and everyone is rewarded or punished appropriately. Realistic fiction in the late nineteenth century rejected these neatly tied up packages of fiction as artificial and mechanical.

But coincidences, deftly handled, are sources of surprise and delight. Writers who want to preserve the magical elements of storytelling continue to make use of this tradition with energy and imagination. E. L. Doctorow, in *Ragtime,* has the lives of his characters crisscross over decades. Thomas Pynchon's *The Crying of Lot 49* makes coincidence its subject.

See *Beginnings, Poetic Justice, Premise, Suspension of Disbelief.*

▼

COMEDY

o   If you want to write comic fiction, you have to learn how to be funny on paper. That might sound obvious, but this is what I mean. When you're writing, you don't have the voice of W. C. Fields to turn an ordinary line like "I'd rather be in Philadelphia" into a piece of American culture.

You don't have Jack Benny's stare or Harpo Marx's bizarre pants to make a scene immediately comic.

Consequently the great writers of comic fiction have had to be master stylists. If you look at pieces by Mark Twain, Dorothy Parker, James Thurber, S. J. Perelman, Robert Benchley, or Woody Allen you find they all have a firm control of diction, image, and the rhythms of language. Their phrasing is cadenced so precisely that even the most straightforward sentences become funny. Often their supposed subjects are spectacularly trivial. Sometimes they deliberately let their ostensible points evaporate entirely. The humor is in the style.

Comic novels need even more. They need imaginative verbal humor, a delicately precise style, and highly crafted prose, but they also need heroes, villains, and an engaging plot. They need more substance too. Good comic writers make penetrating social observations and allow insights into human foibles. The richer the social texture and the truer the insights, the greater the success. That was true of Chaucer, of Fielding, of Dickens, and it is just as true today for writers like Tom Sharpe and David Lodge.

How funny does comic fiction have to be? It used to be said that comedies aimed to amuse and ended happily. It's true, comedy can be jovial, and gentle, as in the beloved fiction of P. G. Wodehouse. But Twain's *Huckleberry Finn* and *A Connecticut Yankee in King Arthur's Court* are biting as well as amusing. American comic fiction tends to be serious, satiric, and, often, a bit grotesque. Successful comic novelists like Joseph Heller or Philip Roth make clear from the start that despite exaggerations, jokes, and caricatures, their works will raise issues of some gravity.

Comic plots tend to be basically simple though they may

be embellished with all sorts of convolutions. Your character is trying to get a degree, as in Kingsley Amis's *Lucky Jim*. Or trying to save the ranch, as in Tom Robbins's *Even Cowgirls Get the Blues*. Or creating a bizarre invention that affects the whole world, as in Kurt Vonnegut's *Cat's Cradle*. The plots often have at their heart archetypal battles between the forces of youth, spontaneity, freedom, and goodness versus age, rigidity, authority, and corruption. Out of those conflicts endless variations are spun involving gladsome spirits versus bankers, teachers, judges, ministers, landlords, and other avatars of repression and joylessness.

Cliff-hangers abound as the plot progresses. You do have to keep things moving by continually introducing danger and the possibility of pain. Characters are always being threatened by loss of love, by loss of life, by loss of money, by confusions, by misunderstandings, by spilled soup.

You have great leeway in comic fiction. You can intermingle zany characters and macabre deaths, sentimental lovers and social satire, but you're holding it all together not by character or plot or theme but by style. Above all, if you want to write comedy, remember this—your mother was right: It's not what you say; it's how you say it.

See *Blue Moon, Farce, Satire, Style*.

▼

CONVENTION

○   A literary convention is a feature that readers accept even though it violates what is considered real or probable. In Shakespeare's plays we accept that the characters speak in blank verse. In opera people sing while they are dying. There are all sorts of conventions in fiction, too. In first-person novels, characters like Huck Finn and Holden Caulfield artfully tell the story of their lives and talk to their readers for hundreds of pages.

Conventions liberate fiction. They allow you to tell the ending of a story before the beginning, what occurs before the story begins, or what happens after the story ends. You can move characters in time and space without describing what your characters did in between or how they got there. You can address your readers; you can address yourself.

You establish your own conventions just as you establish your own characters. If you begin by having your characters talking in an obscure sesquipedalian prose, or by interspersing interludes of raunchy vaudeville jokes and catastrophe statistics, readers will accept those strategies. The freedoms you seize license your fiction for its future liberties.

See *Avant-garde, Formula, Metafiction, Premise.*

CRISIS

The crisis is the turning point of the story. In a detective novel, it is the moment, after being confused and baffled, that the detective figures out the real murderer.

Readers might not know when that moment occurs. All they know is that the detective suddenly decides to visit a certain restaurant and order the vichyssoise. Or the crisis might be rendered so that readers experience it as the character does:

> Suddenly it all started to fall into place—the drops of cream on the victim's pants, the potato skins in poor Chevre's pockets—he had not come from the farm, he'd been at Le Cochon de Lait. And there was only one person he could have been with, Pierre Roti.

The crisis may be a recognition, a decision, or a resolution. The character understands what hasn't been seen before, or realizes what must be done, or finally decides to do it. It's when the worm turns. Timing is crucial. If the crisis occurs too early, readers will expect still another turning point. If it occurs too late, readers will get impatient—the character will seem rather thick. Crises occur three-fifths of the way through a remarkably large number of novels.

Since the crisis helps to give the story its shape, a story that has no crisis, no turning point, presents problems. But the crisis can also be conceptualized as a turning point for readers—the moment they come to some deeper understanding of the story. Without that moment there is no story.

See *Aha!, Epiphany, Plot*.

▼

DESCRIPTION

Young readers often think of description as the parts that they can skip. Naive as that may be, that impulse recognizes something crucial—the parts where the colors of the arroyo or the burnished glow of the furniture are described do not seem quite as urgent as:

> She held out the knife in front of her as she was taught by Mateus.

Or:

> Pinot leapt up. "Wow! You call those pajamas?"

But the creation of the physical world is as crucial to your story as action and dialogue. If your readers can be made to see the glove without fingers or the crumpled yellow tissue, the scene becomes vivid. Readers become present. Touch, sound, taste, and smell make readers feel as if their own fingers are pressing the sticky windowsill.

If you don't create evocative settings, your characters seem to have their conversations in vacuums or in some beige nowhere-in-particular. Some writers love description too much. They go on and on as if they were setting places at the table for an elaborate dinner that will begin later on. Beautiful language or detailed scenery does not generate momentum. Long descriptions can dissipate tension or seem self-indulgent. Don't paint pictures. Paint action.

Description should move the story forward just as dialogue and action do. If it's not crucial to the dynamics of the story, description is static. Those are the parts readers feel are skippable. Description is kinetic and important when it provides necessary information or affects the characters in the story as well as the readers.

Begin to think of settings as characters in your story. A character plays against other characters, increasing tension, creating drama, and advancing the plot. A story about a man in a hurricane is about two characters. A story about a stepfather and a boy and a toy store is about three characters. As noted elsewhere, Henry James commented that he could not imagine "a passage of description that is not in its intention narrative." Poe knew that already. Hemingway never forgot it. Make readers feel *where* actions are taking place, whether in the lobby of Radio City Music Hall or in a smoked-eel shop.

Whatever you're describing, readers need a clear visual image. However, too much visual information is confusing.

The mind loses track easily. A brown Naugahyde chair with a long gash in its seat can establish an interior. Big nostrils can make a person. Give one vivid detail, and readers will build the rest.

Good description follows natural physical movements. The single sweep of the eye from head to foot, from basement to roof, from left to right. Otherwise you get confusion or unintentional weirdness:

> The rat's whiskered nose, gray body, long hairless tail, and glittering red eye.

Scene-setting can be deliberately intriguing. A coin shop is described, and readers are beguiled into wanting to know why. What part will this shop play in the story? The description is tantalizing. It's like introducing a mysterious character and not yet revealing what part she will play.

Writers sometimes forget to describe their own characters. They remain mere voices, thoughts, talking heads, not fully people. Make readers aware continually that your characters are warm-blooded creatures with fleshy folds and itching toes. Keep them corporeal and you'll keep them alive.

Description shouldn't be forced. People notice slowly. At first Esther sees that Marvin is fat and seems unfriendly. Later, Esther notices Marvin has a nice smile and small, delicate hands. Often first impressions are modified. Esther observes a timidity in Marvin's eyes suggesting that his brusque manner results more from shyness than hostility. Every time Esther sees Marvin he becomes more interesting. What Esther notices both establishes Marvin and reveals Esther's capacity to observe. Description is not skippable if it is creating character, plot, and action.

See *Character, Motif, Places and Place Names.*

▼

DIALECT

o   First a warning: Do not attempt dialects with which you are not intimately familiar and for which you have not, in some way, paid your dues. Otherwise, you are likely to make a fool of yourself and seem to be a bigot as well.

For dialects you do know well, it is better to concentrate on rendering the rhythms, the architecture, the syntax of the dialect than to try to indicate pronunciation of individual words by changing spellings and using apostrophes. There are several reasons for that. English is orthographically too imprecise, so the misspellings often don't indicate how the word is pronounced. Also misspellings seem to caricature the speakers, 'n fillin' yuh tawk wit' 'postrophes 'n stuff's tew hahd tuh read. A particular offense is eye dialect, like writing *enuff* for *enough,* since it doesn't change the pronunciation but implies that the speaker is ignorant and inferior.

Look at how beautifully Toni Morrison or William Kennedy handles dialect. Twain's Huck reflects on prayer, "So there ain't no doubt but there is something in that thing. That is, there's something in it when a body like the widow or the parson prays, but it don't work for me, and I reckon it don't work for only just the right kind." In Bernard Malamud's *The Assistant,* Morris tells his wife, "Nobody goes in the night to buy a store. The time to go is in the day to see how many customers. If this man comes here he will see with one eye the store is dead, then he will run home." What you can learn from such passages is how delicate touches and the under-standing of the subtler movements of speech will create the dialect in the mind of the reader.

See *Dialogue, Local Color, Profanity / Obscenity,* "Write What You Know."

▼

DIALOGUE

Advice about dialogue generally starts with discussing what your characters say. It might be better to start off with what your characters don't say and the way they don't. How characters sit or stand is as significant as their spoken sentences.

Make your readers hear the pauses between the sentences. Let them see characters lean forward, fidget with their cuticles, avert their eyes, uncross their legs. If you punctuate the dialogue with this kind of information, readers continually visualize the scene. Setting can intensify dialogue too—for instance, a husband and wife shouting at each other in a crowded supermarket.

How you deal with what characters say to each other offers a spectrum of possibilities:

∘∘ *Summary dialogue* ∘∘

This kind of dialogue is the brief report:

Yvonne told him that she wanted a divorce.

The summary form is highly efficient. It takes up little space while suggesting a long conversation, but it doesn't give much sense of the texture of the conversation.

∘∘ *Indirect dialogue* ∘∘

A more detailed way of reporting dialogue is the indirect quotation, which renders the feeling of what was said without directly quoting it:

> Yvonne said that she wanted a divorce, that he was selfish, that he always had been selfish, that he had never, ever thought of what she really wanted, not even the color of the bedroom.

This is both efficient and rich in texture. Readers feel the words and phrases of the conversation and get a sense of the speaker.

∘∘ *Direct dialogue* ∘∘

This is literally and figuratively the most dramatic form. The reader is in the room with the characters and overhears their conversation in real time, as it happens:

> Yvonne said, "I'm through. You can paint the house any damn color you please."

∘∘ *Intermixed dialogue* ∘∘

It's important for you to recognize that you don't have to choose a single method. These dialogue possibilities can be intermingled within a single scene and even a single speech:

> Yvonne listed his faults—too selfish, too domineering, too petty. "And cheap too. You're one of the cheapest big spenders I ever saw." Yvonne unfolded some sheets of long yellow paper and read out loud what the lawyer had told her about equitable property division.

The above example has indirect dialogue, direct dialogue, and summary. You get the feeling of a fairly long conversation within a few lines.

The form for writing dialogue is fairly simple. Most writers follow certain conventions—the advantage is that readers don't notice them because they are so familiar, and they aren't distracted by odd punctuation or forms.

In direct dialogue, each speaker gets his or her own paragraph even if the speech is very short:

> "Who are you?"
> "Who, me?"
> "Yeah, you."

That's not the only way. A single paragraph can have an interchange between people. To emphasize the flow of the scene you might not even use quotation marks:

> Get out of here, she said. I said, No, you go. I live here, it's my lease. She said, Get out, go away, leave me alone. No, I said, I live here, it's my lease. She looked at me, Go Go Go away. No, I said, this is where I live. I sat back down.

Speech tags are a problem at first for writers. They feel self-conscious about the *he said*s and *Mrs. Philpott said*s of dialogue. But readers register them almost subliminally, as they do punctuation. Speech tags don't intrude, and by preventing confusion they help to keep readers in the world of the story. In a two-person conversation it's good to have a speech tag now and then just so readers don't lose track. If more than two people are in the conversation, you need more speech tags:

> "Well, Eva, you want to get something before the show?"
> Damien said.
> "Why don't we eat after."
> "Pizza first. Movies second. Me want pizza," said Frank.

Variations on *said*, like *answered, commented, added, replied, asked, queried, muttered, snarled, roared*, are best used sparingly. They call attention to themselves and sometimes seem strained. Adverbs in speech tags often sound corny—she said *kittenishly*, he responded *sneeringly*, she hissed *angrily*.

An economical and effective way of tagging speech is to follow the line of dialogue with an action or a thought by the speaker:

> "I'm surprised you came here." Frank jumped up from his chair.
> "I am too." Eva looked past Frank, out the window, as if she did not want to admit that they were in the same room.

Speech tags or action tags can occur at the beginning, in the middle, or at the end of a piece of dialogue. The rhythm of the speech should guide where it goes:

> Velma looked over her desk. "Oh well. What is it now?"

> "A jerk like you," Castor said, "is a diamond a minute."

> "I've got it right here." Tracy opened the drawer and took out a blue envelope.

When you let characters speak—and in your first drafts characters might speak a great deal—they can surprise you with what they have to say. But as you shape your story and revise it, you must be conscious of the impressions and information you want to leave with your readers. So here are some general principles.

Dialogue works best when it is most like real speech rhythms. If the dialogue is not convincing, the character isn't convincing. If readers can't believe in the talk, they won't believe in the talker.

People speak variously. Some talk in clichés, some talk like the authors of philosophy tomes. Some people slip back and forth between dialect and formal language. Writers can signal that they know that the character's speech is idiosyncratic:

> Proget was a weird mix of garret and gutter. One minute he'd be holding forth about post-modern discontinuities and the next he'd be asking if you noticed the receptionist's bazooms.

The result is that readers accept the peculiarity of the speech and, in fact, see it as a distinctive feature that helps establish the character.

Dialogue in which political or philosophical issues are being discussed can also present problems. Readers often feel that the writer is manipulating the discussion in order to set forth certain ideas. For some novelists that's true: They aren't much interested in being realistic, or in moving plot forward. They are using fiction to deploy ideas, and dialogue is one part of the arsenal. If the thoughts are profound, the dialogue witty, or the prose passionate, readers accept the convention and will be patient. Writers like Aldous Huxley, George Orwell, and Saul Bellow have depended more on the strength of their ideas than on their narrative skills. But it's a strategy, not a virtue. Without sufficient eloquence, it's a strategy likely to misfire into tendentiousness.

Dialogue is not a particularly good medium for exposition. If dialogue is forced to carry information that is known to the other characters, it sounds false. It's better to move such information into the character's thoughts or to the narrative voice. Then let the character say what comes naturally.

Some writers use too much direct dialogue. When you use direct quotation you imply that what's being said and how it's said are important. If the characters talk on and on but they're not talking about anything significant, nothing dramatic is happening, and the language isn't distinctive, readers' interest flags. Narrative momentum falters. Too much dialogue also flattens the emotional landscape. If characters talk four pages about their omelet and four pages about their divorce, major scenes and minor scenes feel pretty much alike.

Sometimes writers *want* to render dialogue that is boring, banal, and superficial in order to show that the characters are prigs, mindless sheep, or pretentious fools. But don't write pages of mindless dialogue to prove the characters are mindless. A few sharply chosen examples can suggest a character's pomposity, thoughtlessness, or inanity. F. Scott Fitzgerald, Ann Beattie, and Frederick Barthelme write such dialogue with surgical precision.

Arguments are most nerve-wracking when the characters imply what they feel instead of coming right out and saying it. In fact, the more intense the feelings, the more likely people are to say the opposite of what they really mean. If you want to keep up a high level of tension, keep the dialogue evasive, filled with suppressed information and unstated emotions. Once people really are candid, once the unstated becomes stated, the tension is released, and the effect is cathartic. If you're trying to build pressure, don't take the lid off the pot.

Good dialogue moves the plot forward. If you have a scene showing that Brenda and Joe squabble over nothing, and then another scene showing the same thing, the story feels static. It might be true to life, but readers think, What's the point here? You already told me that.

When you want Brenda finally to tell Joe what a totally insensitive jerk he was the time she had to go to the hospital for some tests, and Joe finally to tell her that he can't stand how she puts him down in company, you want to give yourself the space for a major scene. Here you do want to describe setting and action vividly, and render what they say fully. You've taken the lid off the pot and we want to feel the dialogue boil over.

Dialogue can be persuasion, invasion, evasion, and explosion. Dialogue can be silence.

See *Character, Dialect, Iceberg, Scene.*

▼

DICTION

Diction means word choice. It's the difference between *red* and *carmine, pigheaded* and *obdurate.* Style and voice are created in part by word choices. Direct, simple words get readers involved in the story without drawing attention to the narrator.

> Cara walked into her closet. She took out three pairs of shoes. The black pumps she put on. The running shoes she

put in her handbag. The ballet slippers she pushed down into the front pockets of her jeans. She was ready.

Writers like Ernest Hemingway and Raymond Carver relied on the power of spare, precisely clipped diction.

Exotic words and convoluted syntax draw attention to your presence as narrator and maker of the story.

> Cara's closet, incandescent with the liquid fall of her clothing (Ah, bright fall, fortunate fall!), breathed cognac velours, thin gin strapless gowns, bright frocks of mescal and arak. She elected a water-white silk so slippery, so deceptive, so elusive, so undependable, so perfidious, that it would insouciantly slide off her shoulders and ebb up her thighs with the most blameless, casual, and innocent of movements. Cara licked her lips.

You need to decide if this is the narrator you want to be. Diction strained by circumlocution can suggest self-conscious writers who hide gut feelings behind big words. Some writers fall in love with their own words, and sacrifice their stories on the altar of their ingenuity. But a writer like Vladimir Nabokov makes arcane and esoteric diction part of the richness of his fictional world.

See *Narrator, Psychic Distance, Style, Texture.*

▼

DIDACTICISM

○ Didacticism refers to works that are written primarily to teach and to preach. They might be about the evils of liquor, the futility of war, or the redemptive power of a religious or political system. Or they can have homier moral points, like warning about the bad things that happen if you talk back to Mom. Didactic works tend to have villains who show bad values, heroes who demonstrate good values, long speeches, and a plot that proves the writer's point. Readers generally react negatively when they sense that stories are set up for propaganda purposes, though they're more forgiving when they agree with the ideas. That still doesn't make it good fiction. If you want to move an audience to a certain point of view, remember that the story that maintains its own complexity and integrity will be the most persuasive.

See *Allegory, Fable, Parable.*

▼

DOCUMENTS/DIARIES/LETTERS

○ You can give your fiction immediacy, authenticity, and variety by creating material that is written or read by characters in the story.

Passages from diaries can reveal private selves, intimate fears, or unspoken secrets. Because they are written by characters, they can reveal their sensitivity and level of learning and literacy:

> I hate her. She's so mean. She wont let me ware her cloths and if I get cot stealing them she hits. She dont know what I know about her and if she did shed be singing a difernt song.

Or:

> I wish I could express myself eloquently, but my lips seem to freeze. Everything I would say seems stupid and obvious.

And so we sit silently, our present lives choked by our
unhappy past. I feel so sad, so paralyzed. Why can't I tell
G. how sorry I am? What is not in me?

Letters can be revealing in another way, as your character
presents himself privately to particular others—the face he
shows to his loved one, his mother, or his friends back home.
The juxtaposition of letters with disparate views creates ironies and tensions:

Dear Mom and Dad,
The camp is terrific. Good swimming. Great courts. My
serve is getting great. Met a nice guy named Louis from
Atlanta who is showing me how to hit curves. Food isn't
like yours but at least there's enough of it.

Hey Mannio
I hate this damn place. Nothing but dorks and a million
rules. The counselors are either queers or nazis who hassle
you all the time. Only good thing is sneeking over to the
girls side at night. I can't believe the stuff they let us do.

Dear Natalie
Gosh, I miss you so much. Nothing much going on. At least
I'm getting a good tan. I can't wait to get back this fall.
Gotta go now.

Whole novels have been written as letters, like Samuel Rich-
ardson's *Pamela*, Laclos' *Les Liaisons Dangereuses*, or Lee
Smith's *Fair and Tender Ladies*.

   Newspaper articles, magazine pieces, radio news bulletins,
and advertisements allow you to present other dimensions of

experience—the disembodied public voices of the media. A newspaper article or an obituary makes clear how an event enters history, and might contrast sharply with the story you tell. Headlines or radio news bulletins place the story in time, create atmosphere, and develop tension.

Whatever your documents, keep them relatively brief, or break the passage up by interspersing action. Readers have notoriously short spans of attention. If you want the character (and readers) to notice a single sentence or paragraph, you don't need to cite the whole text. Make sure your documents don't become roadblocks.

See *Style, Tour de Force, Voice.*

▼

ENDINGS

○ In some older fiction the ending was characterized by rewards, punishments, and exciting revelations. In contemporary fiction the tendency is to avoid surprises and symmetry and to recognize that the story must tell itself all the way through.

Endings in short stories are often muted. The story has already made its point or it's not successful. The principle of physics made immortal by Archimedes, "If I had a lever long enough and a place to stand, I could move the world," is instructive. The closer and closer you get to the ending, the more weight every word has, so that by the time you get to the last several words each one carries an enormous meaning. A single gesture or image at the end can outweigh all that has gone before. Choose each word carefully—even simple words like *dark* or *down, light* or *up* drastically affect the sense of the ending and therefore the entire story. Anything revelatory or portentous at the end of the story is very heavy indeed. Heavy-handed, in fact, is the way it's likely to come out.

In beginning the story certain tensions, ideas, and characters have been launched. These themes then fly in intricate formations. The ending doesn't have to provide a surprise. All it has to do is land safely.

Some ingenious writers deploy a number of different themes or characters. Readers are puzzled—these parts seem so disparate, what do they have to do with each other? The ending is the magical moment when the balls thrown in the air all end up in the hand of the writer, and we see, ah, it's one story after all. Flannery O'Connor's "Good Country People" starts by depicting two ignorant older women. Halfway through, the focus of the story moves to an itinerant Bible salesman and the educated daughter of one of the women. Not until we hear the comments of the older women in the last two paragraphs do we understand how the story is all of a piece. But it's not a surprise; it's not an introduction of new information—it's a safe landing. It lets us see what has been there all along.

There's a classic theater story that tells us something very important about endings. An experienced writer was brought in to watch and then revise the ending of a troublesome play that was in rehearsal. "The trouble with the last act," the writer said, "is the first act."

At first that sounds as if he was saying that the whole play was a mess. But there's another meaning in that phrase that's particularly useful for writers of fiction. An ending that seems unsatisfactory might actually be fine. The trouble with the ending might be that the beginning or the middle doesn't set up the ending. A problem scene may not be a problem because of the way it is written, but because of the way some preceding scene is written. The revision of the ending might need to be carried out back in the beginning of the story.

Writers of novels sometimes nervously feel that endings must be very emotional or violent, and go for melodramatic effects. They fear that if there is no major physical confrontation, no grand scene, readers will say, "Is that all? Have you taken me all this way for this?" But if the journey's been worth going on you don't need an earthquake to make it interesting. Many "spectacular" endings seem false to the landscape of the rest of the book. It might be best to stay true to the terms of the fictional world that you made.

Another unsatisfying ending occurs when a writer keeps implying that something really big is going to be revealed. The problem then is that the writer has to live up to it. Otherwise the ending is anticlimactic. The longer you withhold a secret the more likely it is to be disappointing. That's what makes many mystery novels ultimately unfulfilling. What you find out in the end turns out to be something you guessed, or didn't guess—but despite the excitement, it doesn't make much real difference one way or another.

The end of a piece of fiction might be an ambivalent stare or a shattering showdown. What matters is keeping your work true to itself. You start writing the ending when you write your first word.

See *Beginnings, Catharsis, Poetic Justice.*

▼

EPIGRAM

○ These are pithy, witty observations involving clever turns of phrase. Oscar Wilde's characters are memorable because of their turns of phrase and witty *aperçus*.

A narrator can be epigrammatic too. It's a powerful way of establishing an authoritative tone. Readers know that the narrator is a distinct personality who is free to comment on various characters or make observations about life in general. Don't confuse *epigram* with *epigraph*, which refers to those quotations some writers like to put in the front matter of their novels and stories.

See *Narrator, Point of View, Style.*

▼

EPILOGUE

○ This is a good old-fashioned device at the end of a work, allowing authors to tell what happened to the characters after the story is over. William Thackeray concludes *Vanity Fair* with a chapter entitled "Which Contains Births, Marriages, and Deaths." Lately the epilogue is not very much in fashion in serious fiction. It probably fell out of favor since readers liked it so much. But it is always susceptible to revival. See, for example, Margaret Atwood's clever final chapter for *The Handmaid's Tale.*

See *Endings, Frame Story.*

▼

EPIPHANY

○ The epiphany is the moment when the major character comes to some sort of profound realization. It may be an insight into self, into another person, or into the nature of a relationship. It may be psychological, political, philosophical, or theological. It may have comic or tragic consequences. James Joyce, who is responsible for making *epiphany* a widely used concept in modern criticism, wrote about how a seemingly trivial moment can be felt as a "spiritual manifestation" that transforms a character. The sacred connotation of *Epiphany*, meaning God's appearance in the world, suggests the significance of the moment of insight, even when it refers, as it often does now, to personal and secular revelation. Since the epiphany is often the point upon which the whole story turns, it's crucial that readers feel it as a powerful emotional experience.

See *Aha!, Crisis, Objective Correlative, Scene.*

▼

EPISODE

An episode is an incident within a larger narrative. A well-written episode has its own shape—its own beginning, middle, and end. At the same time it advances the plot and contributes to the work as a whole. Writers have problems when they write episodes that are exciting or entertaining or moving in themselves but don't really add much to the story. The question to ask yourself is this: Has the episode, regardless of its virtues, changed the situation significantly for my readers or for my characters?

The adjectival form, *episodic*, is a negative term meaning that the narrative consists of a number of stories, rather loosely related to one another, that don't develop an accumulated power. Something happens and then something else happens and then something else, but no shape is created. Consequently you'll hear readers say, "I enjoyed it, but I never finished it."

See *Stories within Stories*.

▼

EXPOSITION

○　Exposition is the technique used to embed the information you need to tell your story. Readers must know if the year is 1989 or 1898, if the place is Crete or Coral Gables, if the characters are grown-ups or children.

Writers deal with exposition in a variety of ways. Some are perfectly straightforward, starting with a clear statement about the background and situation of a character:

> In the village of Pipik, about four miles from us, there was a butcher named Goddle who had one arm. He had never married, but now he was thirty-five and thought it was time.

Other writers let information leak into the narrative:

> Goddle heaved a rack of ribs onto the chopping block. He sighed. He knew people didn't like to look at him. "A one-armed butcher?" they'd say. "Could that be good luck?" And he knew what they whispered, "Whatever happened to the other arm?" And they'd touch their fingers to the side of their nose as if they knew something.

Both methods have strengths. The first can sound authoritative and convincing, as if the writer were a journalist or historian. The second immediately places readers inside the story.

Some writers have problems because their exposition lacks clarity:

> Robin and I went down to the pool. I was excited because I knew I wasn't allowed to be there without adults, I wasn't allowed to be there at night, and most important, I wasn't allowed to be with Robin by myself.

If readers aren't sure about the age or even the sex of the characters, they can't see the characters and the story seems vague.

Other writers overload their sentences with exposition:

> John Twight stared at the appellate brief he was working on in his two-story brick home in Chapel Hill, North Carolina. Since being brought up in a farming family outside of Boone, graduating cum laude from Davidson College, and going to Harvard Law School he'd often faced difficulties, but this was going to be a tough one to win.

When exposition is intrusive, or sounds as if it is being introduced artificially, the story suffers. That's particularly true for dialogue:

> "I know ever since your King Charles spaniel puppy, Lucifer, got run over by a car, and your goldfish, Gabriel, leapt out of the bowl and died in the dust, you've been mournful, Sharon. So let's go to the pet store downtown."

Sometimes it's not clear what exposition is necessary until after a first draft is complete and you've discovered the story you really want to tell.

See *Beginnings, Dialogue, Endings, Flashback, Tension.*

▼
FABLE

○ This term generally means a short tale—often inhabited by animal characters or in some other way disregarding the ordinary laws of reality—whose point is often summed up in a proverb. Fables need to be felicitously rendered right from the beginning, or they are like those tedious jokes that you suffer through in hopes that the punchline will be adequate recompense.

James Thurber managed to be witty enough, both in the telling and in his parodic epigrams, to make the form work. His fables "The Unicorn in the Garden" and "The Owl Who Was God" are full of verbal play:

> "Can you give me another expression for *that is to say* or *namely*?" asked the secretary bird. "To wit," said the owl.

But they also make sharp moral observations:

> You can fool too many of the people too much of the time.

Fables can easily seem preachy, platitudinous, and portentous. To avoid those pitfalls you need freshness, wit, vitality, and a particularly beguiling style.

See *Didacticism, Epigram, Parable.*

▼
FAIRY TALE

○ A fairy tale is a short story with supernatural elements, usually thought of as part of a folk tradition handed down from one generation to the next. The great collections by Charles Perrault, the Grimm brothers, and Hans Christian Andersen have made such characters as Prince Charming and Cinderella indelible parts of our culture. Writers like John Ruskin and Oscar Wilde, attracted by the freedom from realism in the form, have written their own fairy tales (*King of the Golden River* and "The Happy Prince"). It takes not only a lively imagination, but also a delicate prose hand and a rigorous sense of skepticism to keep fairy tales from becoming sentimental, sententious, or merely precious. Angela Carter wittily creates feminist versions of such traditional stories as "Beauty and the Beast."

See *Style, Suspension of Disbelief.*

▼

FARCE

○   Farce is a form of comedy that allows exaggerations, improbabilities, slapstick, old jokes, bad puns, and caricatures. On the stage, pure farce approaches ballet in its demand for exquisite timing, dancelike movements, and gymnastic clowning. In fiction, farce can be similarly effective, as in some of the novels of Joyce Cary or Tom Sharpe.

You need an uninhibited and zany imagination, and you also need to establish your settings and props with great care. When the Volkswagen is sliding backward into the lake that contains an ancient but demented alligator, and your hero is trying to crank open the stubborn sunroof to escape, *readers need to know already* that his girlfriend, who broke off their relationship because of a misunderstanding about the odd shape of his suntan, is a scuba diver who searches lake beds for the fossil coprolites of ancient marsupials. In farce especially, you need to have all the ducks in a row before you can make them quack.

Farce is also used negatively to mean that the comedy has gotten too exaggerated and readers no longer believe in the author's fictional world. Writers can be seduced by their own outrageous ideas. There is no exact answer to how far you can go, but your characters have to be kept in character—they need to retain their human complexity, even underwater.

See *Comedy, Premise.*

▼

FLASHBACK

○ The flashback is a way of telling stories that happened before the story you are telling. It's a vivid way of getting information to readers about your character's past. It's also a totally natural device. Flashes from your own past continually occur in the present. You look at a car in traffic and it reminds you of your first car, and that may remind you of the time you skidded in the snow, abandoned it, and slogged to the Amoco station and drank hot chocolate. The flashback takes place in an instant.

Flashbacks work well when they are brief, vivid, and narrative in form. Tell a recalled anecdote as a miniature story, with the same attention to proportion and detail as the main line of action. Since we don't have total recall of direct dialogue, use dialogue sparingly, and only when the exact phrase is of importance. Indirect dialogue is more efficient. Return to the main line of action as quickly and crisply as possible. You can tell a long flashback in segments, but writers who let flashbacks run on for pages risk losing momentum. Readers

say, "Get on with it. Tell the story. Stop this endless rumi-
nating. No more flashbacks."

Since flashbacks are a natural way of thinking, the entry
points for them are not hard to find. Whatever your character
comes across—a leaky ballpoint pen, a Campbell's soup can,
a shouting garbageman—can be a trigger for a flashback.

Flashbacks give history, depth, and texture. They convey
what no one else can see, what no one else knows. That intimate understanding makes readers more, not less, engaged in
your story.

See *Character, Episode, Immediacy, Interior Monologue,
Motif, Stories within Stories.*

▼

FORMULA

Formula is a negative term suggesting that the
plot or idea is too old, too familiar, and too contrived. James
N. Young's *101 Plots Used and Abused* is a horribly delight-
ful collection of formula stories that editors have seen far too
often—dozens of variations on the guy who commits the perfect crime but forgets one little thing, or the crooked manu-
facturer who makes a shoddy product and then his life depends
on it working (and it doesn't), or the outraged character who
carries out some terrible revenge on the wrong person. A formula story calls attention to itself as a remarkable and ingenious plot, when really it is old straw.

In themselves, natural formulas are basic elements in the
chemistry of fiction. A *worm turns* plot, in which a character
discovers his strength and does what he could not do before,
occurs in literature from *The Iliad* to *The Little Engine That
Could.* It's found so often because the struggle to overcome

obstacles is part of universal experience. In fiction certain plots echo similarly ubiquitous events, such as *girl meets boy, girl loses boy, girl gets boy.* The detective novel's *unorthodox detective is suspected of crime, but ultimately finds real killer* expresses the widespread fantasy of vindication from false accusation and triumph over unjust authority.

In the negative sense, formula writing ultimately means that the writer has not created a rich, individual world, has not put in enough energy, has not made something new and alive, so the bare bones of the formula show.

See *Cliché,* "Don't Do This," *Genre, Irony, Plot, Stereotype.*

▼

FRAME STORY

A frame story is a story within a story. In a classic frame you have a character tell a story, usually to another character or to a group of listeners. This device is popular for tales of supernatural or otherwise difficult-to-believe events. It's also a way of assembling many stories under one title. Boccaccio's *Decameron* has ten characters, each telling ten stories over the ten days they spend together. Some frame stories complicate matters by having a storyteller tell a story about a storyteller telling a story and so on in the manner of Chinese boxes.

The frame story also has the distinction of being one of the oldest and most clichéd of fictional forms:

> It was a dark and stormy night and all the men were gathered around the campfire and the captain said, "Julius, tell us a story." And Julius said, "It was a dark and stormy night . . ."

In sophisticated frame stories, the teller is not simply a narrative device, but someone with a psychologically complex relation to the tale. In Joseph Conrad's *Heart of Darkness,* Marlowe tells a story about the terrifying adventures of Kurtz. But Marlowe's telling reveals how his own life was changed by what happened to Kurtz. There is a subtle psychological relationship between the frame and the picture—that relationship turns out to be the real story.

The frame story can be useful in other ways. An adult narrator can recall childhood experiences. Since your teller is older, he can have reflections, memories, and psychological distance. At the same time, what you put in the frame has immediacy:

> I was just eight that summer. I didn't realize it then but my parents must have silently decided to drink themselves to death, and only got up from their blue recliners to call Buford's for more vodka and beer. My brother, who was eleven, would go off and leave me in other people's yards. That's how I met Matilda. It was not until many years later that I began to understand what happened to all of us.

Your frame can create a transition to the past, to the future, or to strange other worlds. Writers like Robert Louis Stevenson and Somerset Maugham liked the way frames combine distance and immediacy. It's an old-fashioned device, and therefore particularly interesting today as we explore layers of fictionality.

Other stories need no frame at all. A swift beginning plunges readers into the midst of action. Writers often think they need to frame when they really do not. You ought to try unframing your framed stories and see how they look bare. They might surprise you and your readers.

See *Beginnings, Blue Moon, Metafiction, Narrator, Point of View, Premise.*

▼

FREYTAG'S PYRAMID

ο   This classic description of rising and falling action that characterizes most successful fiction, particularly longer works, was formulated by a nineteenth-century German novelist, playwright, and critic.

Gustav Freytag identified key elements. First, readers feel they must know who is in the story and where and when it is taking place (*exposition*); the plot has to get going early (*rising action*); once readers understand the situation, something else has to happen to keep things going (*complication*); and all this leads to something (*climax*) where things change (*reversal*), and as things wind down (*falling action*) the end is reached (*catastrophe*).

Although Freytag was focusing on drama, if you're writing a novel, you should consider the strength of this structure. One way or another, crudely or subtly, it underlies most fiction. You can modify it by changing the order, fragmenting pieces, eliminating others, and otherwise warping, exploding, imploding, or ingeniously stressing a single element. Faulkner's exposition in *The Sound and the Fury* is through Benjy, a character who has no adult understanding of what he says. The rising action and climax in Nabokov's *Pale Fire* occur in footnotes. But these writers understood that you can't hold up a bridge with a smile—distorting, inverting, or undoing traditional structure meant that they had to discover other ways to keep immediacy, tension, and momentum.

See *Novel, Plot, Position, Suspense, Tension.*

▼

GENRE

o   For fiction, *genre* means specific categories like science fiction, fantasy, horror, espionage, detective, Western, romance, young adult. There are also subgenres like erotic romance, quiet horror, and police procedural. The principles and rules that govern each genre can be quite specific.

Writing successful genre fiction demands serious professional craftsmanship. You need to know the genre to get a feeling for its demands. These demands include such matters as optimum length, best ages for main characters, desired number of subplots, satisfactory endings, and so forth. There are many helpful manuals and guides available.

If you try to do original or striking work that violates the genre, there can be a serious marketing problem. Genre publishers may not feel comfortable with the manuscript because their readers tend to have certain expectations. Non-genre publishers may return the manuscript because to them it looks like a genre book.

Some writers, though they neither enjoy nor know much about a genre, will cynically try to turn out a romance or a Western. The effort usually ends up being a waste of time; their lack of belief in what they're doing shows through.

A sellable genre novel has to have its own freshness, its own originality, its own integrity. Character, dialogue, description, and plot must be energetic and captivating. Within its particular galaxy, the genre novel must create a world.

See *Cliché,* "Don't Do This," *Melodrama, Science Fiction.*

▼

GROTESQUE

○ The term is used in literary criticism to refer to incongruous, bizarre, and abnormal characters and events. As far back as we can remember, literature has always been peopled with the abnormal, with giants, monsters, and unworldly creatures. Dickens's grotesque characters are often physically repulsive. Sherwood Anderson focused specifically on psychological distortion. Flannery O'Connor stressed spiritual deformation.

It's best not to set out consciously to be grotesque. Create your characters truly, fully, and fearlessly, and let the critics worry about what category of grotesquerie, if any, they might inhabit. If you set out to create grotesque effects, your fiction is likely to come across as artificial and self-conscious. If the world you "know" is, in reality, grotesque, then your fiction will be naturally unnatural—its strangeness not unbelievable but as convincing as a cross-town bus.

See *Blue Moon, Character, Realism.*

▼

HERO

○ The hero—the traditional term for the protagonist, central figure, or main character—has almost vanished from serious literary conversation. We don't much believe in heroes, especially in the original classical sense of humans who consort with the gods and often have supernatural powers themselves. The very phrase "our hero" has been ironic for a long time.

Whatever you call this character, however, one principle holds: The more pages to the fiction, the more absorbing the hero has to be. The reasons are inescapable. The longer it takes to read the book, the more readers need to feel empathy, sympathy, and curiosity about your character. Whether your hero is sensitive or single-minded, brainy or brawny, shrewd or reckless, *your readers have to care.*

If your hero character, and let's say the hero is a woman, is psychologically attractive—a person of integrity, energy, and force (with a few human flaws)—readers will side with her and be appropriately angry at those who don't treat her well. Readers are drawn to energy, to the mix of tough and tender, to good values, and to attractive idiosyncrasies.

If your hero is seriously flawed, she has to be particularly interesting. Underneath it all, she needs to be insightful or funny or sensitive enough to stay fascinating. Your other characters make their entrances and exits, but your hero is with those readers chapter after chapter. Readers must feel that they are always learning more about her. They must develop a sense of kinship. They might be irritated or scared by what she does, but if they understand what she's going through, they'll walk in her Birkenstocks.

See *Anti-hero, Character, Picaro.*

▼

IMAGERY

o   Imagery, in writing, is the technique of using language, particularly figures of speech such as similes and metaphors, to create emotions and sensations. For example, Stephen Crane starts *The Red Badge of Courage* by saying that the army "awakened" and "cast its eyes upon the road" and that a stream runs "at the army's feet." His imagery turns the army into a single animal.

Imagery induces readers to see things in certain ways. If you keep comparing your characters to weapons, you'll influence your readers to think of war:

> Garth's eyes glinted like bullets. Ramona's voice was like shrapnel.

If you change the imagery you change the meaning:

> Ramona's hair was the color of burnished mahogany.

Or:

> Ramona's hair was the color of beef liver.

The issue is not the shade of brown Ramona's hair happens to be. You choose the image that creates the sensation you want.

Imagery affects form and meaning. Continually referring to dark colors, or things from nature, or machinery, creates a subtle pattern that unifies the work, and suggests themes that the reader feels, often without fully realizing why.

Lyrical imagery sets up other expectations—seriousness, emotion, and intensity:

We stood shivering and wet, watching the aspen's leaves tremble like Bible pages in the rising gale.

Raw images that conjure up pictures of pain and violence suggest a brutal world and the possibility of a dark ending:

The wind punched mean and dirty. Tree branches whined, whimpered, and cracked like broken arms.

Fanciful imagery suggests a world where anything might happen:

The hurricane roared like a sound system cranked too high, and the trees were all slamdancing with the aspens doing some kind of weird hula. Pines were bending, poplars were wiggling, birches were touching the ground. It was be-bop hurricane Saturday night, and we were invited to the party.

Controlling your imagery is important. If you start out with morbid images and those references then disappear, it's as if you introduced a character and forgot about him in the middle of the story. If your imagery mainly involves birds and flowers, an image suggesting that "Geoffrey looked like a Martian with a hangover" is incongruous.

See *Cliché, Diction, Metaphor and Simile, Motif, Style, Texture.*

▼

IMAGINATION

"Use your imagination," people will tell you. But what is imagination? The trouble is, when people are told to use their imagination, they often fail to call on their own imagination. They use Tolkien's or Walt Disney's, Stephen King's or George Lucas's, the world of James Bond or *Miami Vice.* Doing this almost seems the opposite of "Use your imagination."

Imagination really means unleashing your personal experience, your own fears and nightmares. Let those memories and thoughts run free and see where they go, what jungles they'll inhabit, what lairs they create. Tolkien's world came out of his personal fascination with the English language. Stephen King's came from his own childhood obsessions. Using your imagination means diving into what makes you different from everyone else, not what makes you the same.

See *Blue Moon, Trust Your Material,* "Write What You Know."

▼

IMMEDIACY

○ When your readers feel that they are really *there*, that the narrative is happening right in front of them, you've achieved immediacy. Immediacy comes from sharp description, crisp dialogue, and vivid action.

Whether you use first, second, or third person, you still want to create immediacy. Present tense intensifies the sense that the action is going on at that moment:

> I jump up and grab the fat tree branch. The bark scales my hands and I lock my fingers together over the top. I hang straight down and start to swing my legs forward and back.

> You swing until you feel the blood going out to your feet and filling your shoes. Your hands don't feel real anymore, as though they're hooks holding you to the tree.

Dexie keeps swinging, letting his body go numb and rigid, like he's a pendulum, a piece of wood, if he just keeps his hands locked, he'd be part of the tree, never have to let go, never have to touch the ground again.

But past tense can be just as successful in creating immediacy:

I felt as long as I hung there I was just me, and not my family, not my little brother yelling, "Leave it alone, leave it alone!" Not my sister with the scissors saying, "Shut up, they're not supposed to have ears," and the puppy yipping from under the house, too smart to come out.

You just stood there, too afraid of her, not only the scissors in her hand but her mouth that would call you a sissy and stupid and a baby, and you'd somehow know it was true even though you were older than she was.

Dexie hung until he thought his interlocked fingers had melted together; his scraped wrists felt like stretched rubber and his arms had become straight sticks. He felt as though he couldn't let go if he wanted to; his head lolled forward like a man hanging from his own gallows. He looked down at his floating shoes, untied laces, and the dirt below, and swayed slowly.

Flashbacks need to have a similar immediacy:

I remembered when my father had shown me insects caught in spiderwebs. In our red plaid jackets, we'd squat together in the tall wet grass, and he'd put one arm around my shoulder and point with the other into the depths of the bushes. He'd steady me, pull me close, and turn my shoulders so I could see what he saw. I'd nestle into the wet wool and my eyes would follow his stubby finger to the tiny, silvery webs.

You saw glinting minute flies enmeshed in thin filaments, some still vibrating their almost invisible wings, and you'd see the spiders, sometimes even smaller than their prey. They'd dash out from darkness, run along a thin strand, circle the buzzing insect, then climb round and round him, as if wrapping string on a ball.

Dexie remembered how his father wanted him to marvel at the spider, at his purposeful movements, and perhaps to have pity for the prey. He wanted Dexie to understand it's all nature, it's all natural. But what fascinated Dexie was neither spider nor fly—it was the web, the thing made, its silvery shape, sometimes like a funnel or a net but often more like a haze of light.

Immediacy is possible even when you deal with long stretches of time. In his trilogy *U.S.A.* John Dos Passos encapsulates a childhood, the years of high school, or a stint in the military in single paragraphs. But the rhythm of his sentences and his attention to specific images and single details give those sections as much immediacy as fully rendered scenes.

See *Mise-en-scène, Scene.*

▼
INTERIOR MONOLOGUE

○ Interior monologue lets your readers know what your character is thinking. The reader is inside the character's head, rather than learning about the character in a simple summary like:

> Viktor was ambitious, unscrupulous, and oddly self-righteous. He was determined to marry her and thought he deserved to.

The term *interior dialogue* might be clearer than *interior monologue*. You can render the back-and-forth movement of the character's thoughts and feelings and fears and memories, as if a drama were taking place in his head.

> Viktor felt baffled. He had tried whimpering about how depressed he was, how badly treated by his sister, his mother, his so-called boss, and what had she said? "Stand up for yourself." Stand up? Who did she think she was? She should be flattered that he would court her, that he pretended to show his vulnerability. Didn't she realize his confiding to her was an honor? It was almost enough to make him abandon his project.

When you enter a character's mind, your readers are truly getting to know him from the inside. You are going beyond what someone *does* to who someone *is*.

How many characters can be created from the inside in a single work? If more than one, how do you get from the inside of one head to another? The deeper you go into one character's mind, the more careful the transitions must be. Scale is one determinant. Short stories tend to take place in one mind; novels have more scope.

Henry James liked to stay in one character. Flaubert moved from one character to another, sliding his readers out of one point of view and into another without their realizing it. Novels today often change points of view at the chapter breaks.

See *Character, Flashback, Juggling, Point of View, Stream of Consciousness, Transitions.*

▼

INTRIGANT

An intrigant, a word whose meaning I have somewhat bent (from "one who makes intrigues" to "that which does intrigue"), is any device that keeps readers going.

An intrigant gets the story started in the first place. If you begin with a dog walking down a street with a Bible in its mouth, you hope that you have aroused your readers' curiosity.

Then you need to keep their attention. In longer fiction intrigants are crucial to momentum. If an unstable situation creates interest, readers want to know what happens next. What happens next should generate another instability, another intrigant, which, in turn, makes readers say, "What happens next?" Plot itself is an interlinking of intrigants. Just read Graham Greene.

Information itself can be intriguing by creating the need for more information. If we learn early that Barney had "some trouble" in North Carolina, we want to know what it was. When we learn he was in prison, we want to know what for. When we find out it was for embezzling, we want to know from whom, and how much, and how he got into that. We learn it was because he owed money to someone who "wasn't very nice." Now we want to know who that could be, and why Barney wanted the money. When we learn the money-lender was a Sicilian gangster, and Barney wanted to buy a goat farm, we want to know more about a guy who knows gangsters, is capable of embezzling, and wants to be a goat farmer.

Intrigants can be created through simple phrases. A chapter that ends "But that's not all Sam found out" hooks readers. An unexplained action is an intrigant: "Molly held up a single red sock in her outstretched hand." Or you can use a piece of dialogue: "I'll tell you tomorrow, but I know you're going to hate me." Attention to such details can keep your fiction taut, can keep the reader turning pages.

See *Cliff-hanger, Novel, Plot, Suspense, Tension, Zigzag.*

▼

IRONY

○ Irony refers to the discrepancy between appearance and reality, surface and depth, ignorance and knowledge. Discordance, disagreement, incongruity, difference—all are aspects of irony and all create tension. Fiction dances on tension.

Sarcasm is one form of irony—the discrepancy between what is said and what is meant:

"Thanks a lot. I was hoping someone would drop a piano on my foot."

Irony results when characters don't know something important. For example, Bartlett is bragging about how clever he is while the readers know his car has just been stolen. Irony can be funny or serious, comic or tragic. It can show a character is a fool because he doesn't realize what everyone else at the bar does—the woman he's flirting with is really a man. Or it can show him to be a victim—there was no way he could know that the bank never intended to give him the loan.

Irony can easily get too heavy-handed. That happens when the irony is based on a simple inversion of expectations— Wendy, the sweet, sympathetic guidance counselor, turns out to be the psychopathic killer. It is true that for the audience there is an atavistic delight in the irony of the evil bank manger arrested for embezzlement and the brutal rancher trampled in a cattle stampede. But these ironies are mechanical, they're formulaic, they're too simplistic to take seriously.

Subtle irony occurs when characters don't get exactly what they want but, instead, get something less definite, less predictable, more puzzling. Since that pretty much sums up what happens in life, these more complex ironies characterize contemporary fiction.

There is an interesting relationship between irony and scale. The shorter the work of fiction, the subtler the ironies need to be. Short stories that depend on the irony of simple inversion can easily feel didactic, manipulated, or sentimental. The longer the work, the larger the ironies it can sustain. In Melville's *Moby-Dick* the hunted destroys the hunter, as obvious an irony as you can think of, but that catastrophe brings the book to a magnificent, powerful end. In Stephen Crane's *The Red Badge of Courage*, the hero ultimately believes he's traveled from ignorance to knowledge while Crane makes us see he's traveled from one kind of ignorance to another perhaps greater ignorance.

See *Cliché, Formula, Plot, Poetic Justice, Tension.*

▼
LEGEND

○   A legend is a traditional story often associated with a particular place, person, belief, or custom. It explains why a local mansion is called "Rooster's Curse," or the old man who owns the grocery is known as "Doubledead." With legends you can distance yourself from your narrative, the way you can with a frame story. Readers accept supernatural or strange occurrences as local tradition and aren't put off by problems about their literal truth. Washington Irving did that in "The Legend of Sleepy Hollow" and "Rip Van Winkle." Richard Brautigan updates the technique in *Trout Fishing in America* and *A Confederate General from Big Sur*.

You can make use of legendary material or make up your own legends, but you can't expect readers to be patient with pseudo-folksiness—"I was told this here story by my gran-pappy when I was a young-un"—or with familiar material like ghostly hitchhikers who haunt truckstops. Create tension from the start and develop the story out of its own premises. Don't simply string together inexplicable events. Make readers feel that the story is not merely weird, but deeply mysterious.

See *Fairy Tale, Places and Place Names, Premise*.

▼
LOCAL COLOR

○   Toward the end of the nineteenth century, Americans became curious about regional differences in manners, dress, foods, speech, and rituals. Writers like Sarah Orne Jewett and George Washington Cable produced fiction describing local customs, often focusing on rituals like weddings, holidays, and funerals, or on daily life. They recorded poverty and pain as well as quaintness and joy.

These local-color writers were influential in the development of American fiction. They stressed accuracy of detail, direct observation, and personal experience—writers couldn't describe a Vermont barn-raising or a Tennessee wedding unless they went themselves. They recognized that ordinary people and ordinary lives could make lively fiction, that plots could be simple, that texture and atmosphere could create a story, and that regional, non-standard speech had its own poetry.

They were not revolutionaries. European and British writers were already doing the same thing. Often American local-color writers were sentimental or superficial. But they also included Mark Twain and Kate Chopin. And their influence underlies the work of William Faulkner, William Kennedy, Bobbie Ann Mason, and Toni Morrison. If the local color of the past was usually rural, the local color of the present, captured by writers like Frederick Barthelme, is often urban.

The potential for local color persists, but now it's not so much geographical (the McDonald's-is-everywhere syndrome) as cultural. America is a mosaic of hikers, bikers, sky divers, quilters, stock traders, and Avon salespeople. The American suburb deserves attention. It's perhaps difficult to perceive the cultural peculiarities in front of your own remote-controlled two-car garage, but, to other people, peanut butter on white bread is as exotic as pone.

See *Accuracy, Dialect, Gathering, Onion, Realism,* "Write What You Know."

▼

MELODRAMA

○ Melodrama is a form that is devoted more to creating sensations than to making sense. It manipulates plots and characters for the sake of chills, thrills, sadness, and joy. It can have daring rescues, secret identities, sudden love, complete character changes, and plots so complicated it's sometimes not clear if even the writer has kept them straight.

Naturally, melodrama is terrifically popular.

See *Bathos, Coincidence, Frame Story, Stereotype.*

▼

METAFICTION

○ Metafiction is fiction that plays with the conventions of fiction. Metafiction avoids traditional narrative by unorthodox treatment of time, space, character, and voice, but its most salient characteristic is self-referentiality—it comments on itself as a piece of writing.

Some of the earliest fiction in English, like John Lyly's *Euphues*, was highly self-conscious, but Laurence Sterne's *Tristram Shandy* is the great classic of fiction about fiction. In the novel, Sterne talks to the reader about how the writing is going, explains what he is going to do next, and has chapters that are blank pages to indicate he's not going to tell what went on in them. William Thackeray, Charles Dickens, Henry James, and Gertrude Stein sometimes would comment on their writing within their works. In Flann O'Brien's *At-Swim-Two-Birds* the characters rebel against the author for making them do things they don't like. Alain Robbe-Grillet, Jorge Borges, Donald Barthelme, and William Gass have made good fiction while ingeniously exploding its own conventions. Metafictional devices are not limited to a small intellectual coterie. Richard Brautigan and Tom Robbins have had great popular success with their highly unconventional novels.

See *Avant-garde, Fairy Tale, Legend, Parable, Parody, Premise.*

▼

METAPHOR AND SIMILE

○ Metaphor refers to imagery that describes something by saying it is something else:

> Roger was an egg, his wife, Myrtle, a kind of absentminded duck.

Metaphor is powerful because it can suggest so much in a single word. For example, *egg* makes us think Roger is passive and simple—as unformed as if he weren't born yet. Myrtle as a *duck* implies that she fusses about, wiggles, waggles, and fluffs her feathers. And the silliness of the metaphors tells us to expect a comic story. Witty, folksy, or poetic narrators establish their voice through the appropriate metaphors.

Since metaphor says something *is* something else ("You are my sweet petunia") and simile says something is *as if* it was something else ("You are like a sweet petunia to me"), metaphor is more direct and dramatic. Metaphor creates identity. Simile establishes likeness. That doesn't make metaphor intrinsically superior to simile. Each type of image has its own uses.

Metaphors and similes can enrich your style, but, since they call attention to themselves, they'd better be worth it. They need to be fresh, lively, and pertinent. Be sure they're consistent with your narrative voice. Too many metaphors too close together can cause confusion:

> Arnold and I were oxen in the snow as we pushed the car; our boots were wet fetlocks, as we tried to get the mule-stubborn engine to roar with life, to shepherd us to our expectant families in their warm dens.

The New Yorker has an occasional filler called "Block That Metaphor" citing writers who have extended their metaphors far beyond their grasp.

Too many similes can make your readers feel that you are always saying what things are like instead of what they are:

> Her cheeks were as smooth as watered silk and her deep brown eyes shone like topazes as we walked, on the sand, white as powdered ivory, toward the sun setting like a golden yolk on the dark horizon.

In your first draft don't be inhibited; let the images pour out. In revision, you can figure out which metaphors and similes to toss overboard.

See *Imagery, Style, Texture.*

▼

MISE-EN-SCÈNE

This term, borrowed from drama, refers to the stage setting of a play. It was appropriated by film criticism to mean all that the viewer sees in a single shot. It's also a useful concept when you're writing major scenes in fiction, especially when a number of characters are involved.

Visualize your setting for a major scene. Is it vague? A living room, you say, but have you thought about sofas and lamps and the paintings on the wall? Conversations or actions that aren't placed in a vivid setting seem disembodied. Readers feel a character's weight if there is a couch to plop into or a hassock to kick. Establish the space and the place so he can put his meaty hand on the drapes and bump into the Hepplewhite table.

If you gather characters in a single scene, tension increases dramatically. Two people create two reciprocal relationships (for example, how Adrien treats Button, and how Button treats Adrien). But four people create twelve possible interactions and six create thirty. A roomful of people generates a lot of heat.

See *Description, Scene.*

▼

MOTIF

○ A motif is a recurring element in a work. It can be your character's tendency to sneak drinks out of the slivovitz bottle, a chair shaped like a kidney, worry about paying the rent, or the slugs on the rose bushes. The more often you mention something, the more important a motif it becomes.

A repeated image grows in meaning. If you have your characters complaining over and over about the croaking of the frogs, not only do readers hear the shrill, nerve-racking sound more intensely and feel its effect on the characters more strongly, but also your readers begin to speculate on the thematic significance of the constant noise.

Motifs play a part in plot. The first time June tells Frank

she gets nervous when he leaves the closet door open it's simply information. When Frank leaves the closet door open again, readers aren't surprised that June gets upset. When Frank leaves the closet door open once again, readers feel something more is going on—perhaps Frank is being deliberately cruel. The next time, it's really frightening. The closet door becomes more ominous, more psychologically suggestive, each time it's left open.

Motifs unify stories. The repetition of images darkens or brightens the atmosphere. Motifs bring ideas forward. If you mention the dead geranium only once, it will be forgotten. If you keep mentioning the dead geranium, by the end of the story it will be memorable.

Don't be afraid of repetition. Don't raise an idea and, having raised it, go on to another and another. That doesn't develop a story. If you don't bring ideas forward, they'll just be left behind.

See *Character, Description, Flashback, Imagery, Metaphor and Simile, Theme.*

▼

MYTH

○   Myths address the deepest and oldest questions of humankind—why we exist, how we came to be, and what will happen to us.

Greek, Roman, Norse, and biblical myths were once our cultural heritage. Children's versions of the stories of gods and goddesses were read at bedtime and appeared in the school curriculum. You could expect your readers to know of Leda, Loki, Lazarus, and the Laocoön. Writers made references to myths because a name like *Hercules* could conjure up a whole cycle of adventures. Today, readers tend not to know much about mythology and references to mythological figures may be recognizable to only a few.

But fiction's attempts to answer life's ultimate mysteries haven't gone away, and the pleasure of embedding—through the mention of a name or place—the most profound and enduring stories in the history of humankind is too rich to abandon. Someone will know what you're doing.

Just keep in mind that the story is what makes the mythical allusions work. Allusions by themselves can't give the story life. James Joyce's *Ulysses* is, first, vividly about his Dublin characters. It gains a marvelous resonance by echoing the characters and events of Homer's *Odyssey*. But if we weren't persuaded by the work's immediate vitality and rich texture, we wouldn't be much interested in its intellectual substructure. If you retell the story of Prometheus, you can't rely on the allusion to give fire to your work. You have to set your own fire.

See *Allusion, Archetype, Motif, Theme.*

▼
NAMES

o Some writers have a problem in naming characters. They may choose names like Justinian or Angelique because they like them, even though the names don't suit the characters' backgrounds. Or they believe that the "real-life" character has a name so perfect that they can't imagine any other. Still other writers don't like to think about names and choose the first Tom, Dick, or Mary name that comes to mind.

In fact, creating names is too important to be neglected or treated lightly. Every time you mention the name, you're giving your character body, life, and personality. A subtly suggestive name creates a cluster of impressions. Joseph Serzicki sounds different from Newington Tribble. Names are succinct ways of suggesting a character's ethnic, religious, geographical, and social background. Names tell about parental aspirations—Tiffany Trump, or Percy Shelley Underwood. They tell how much a family is governed by its past (Hamilton Quince), how much it wanted to reject tradition (Purple Hayes), or how much ambivalence there is about its heritage (Kevin Cohen). Give your characters full names. Characters without full names are Ken and Barbie.

Names can have a symbolic and thematic resonance as well. In earlier fiction, names were often overtly meaningful, almost allegorical. The good man in Henry Fielding's *Tom Jones* is Squire Allworthy. The nasty chaplain who believes in corporal punishment is Thwackum. In the twentieth century, that explicitness seems old-fashioned, but names do still suggest ideas. In Nathanael West's *Miss Lonelyhearts* our hero is treated cruelly by the relentlessly cynical Shrike. Thomas Pynchon's questioning heroine in *The Crying of Lot 49* is named Oedipa.

Inspiration for good names is everywhere—in baby-name dictionaries, in obituaries, in circuit court dockets, in phone books, and in literature. But don't appropriate the full real name of a private person. Even if you invent a name, if you say the character is from Ronkonkoma, before publication you'd better make sure no such person lives in Ronkonkoma. Lawsuits have occurred.

Names that are too contrived create their own problems. When the names seem artificial—Arlington Stormdrain or Ozwanne Damme—readers tend to be put off. The unreality of the names undercuts credibility right from the start.

As noted in the section "Don't Do This," writers often unconsciously give characters names that are phonetically and visually similar. Barry and Larry, Kim and Jan. That confuses readers. Names that have different sounds, shapes, and lengths help to differentiate your characters.

See *Character, Places and Place Names.*

▼

NARRATIVE

⚬ A narrative tells what happened. It's the story line in fiction. It's the sequence of events in nonfiction. *Narrative historians* are writers who specialize in telling the story of a culture rather than analyzing the reasons for its rise or fall.

Years ago I heard Isaac Bashevis Singer talking about nineteenth-century psychology books such as Krafft-Ebing's *Psychopathia Sexualis*. He said we all recognize that the medical commentary is completely outdated, uninformed, and ridiculous by our standards. But, he went on to say, the case histories, the stories, the narratives, remain fascinating. They still live; they can never grow old or become dated.

It's a point worth remembering. The heart of fiction remains in narrative. "Tell me a story" is an appeal from our most primeval selves. You can aspire to explore the human heart, to analyze cultural conditions, to propose social reforms, and to discuss philosophical ideas, but if you want to fascinate, to hold on to your readers, make sure you also tell them a good story.

See *Novel, Plot, Short Novel, Short Story, Structure.*

▼

NARRATOR

○ The narrator is the teller of the story. You invent the narrator just as you invent a character. You might want your narrator to be an Italian grandmother, an Israeli taxi driver, or an autistic child. Even if the narrator is much like yourself, you still need to make decisions about voice style, how much the narrator will know about each character, and how insightful you want the narrator to be.

Omniscient narrators are free to tell whatever they want about the characters, even things that may not have happened yet:

> When Harvey Wolf dropped Lisa Caskit's Fourth Grade Reader down the sewer, only Harvey knew it was for love. Lisa went right home and asked her daddy to shoot Harvey. That was love too—though Lisa didn't understand that too clearly. Lisa's dad took her seriously as he did everything in life, and loaded up to go visit the Wolfs. He put on his blue hunting jacket and slipped some extra shells in his pockets.

Your narrator can have *limited omniscience.* You might not want your narrator to understand everything. Sometimes it's more convincing if the narrator admits not knowing the whole story:

> I don't know why Lisa's father decided, while on this mission of revenge, to stop in the town library, a building he

had never entered before, and ask to see a copy of the Fourth Grade Reader. Lisa's father was not a patient man, and he was not a gentle man, but Lowell Caskit had a streak of curiosity.

Objective narrators describe what is externally observable and deducible, but generally refrain from seeing the world through the eyes of other characters. This can be an economical and convincing way to tell a story, for the impression is of someone simply telling what happened so far as he knows it, like a news report of a strange occurrence:

> Lowell Caskit took the book from the librarian and sat near the bay window. He flipped to the middle, read a few pages, and stopped. He stared into the book, then out the window. He looked at another page, and stared again. He rose, returned the book without speaking, and walked toward the door, patting the shells in his pockets.

Foregrounded narrators may be outside the story but they draw attention to themselves by their prose style, commentary, and observations so that readers are always aware of the teller of the story:

> The Caskit family, worn down by time, carried history as a fox carries a snake in his teeth. Once Casquette or, possibly, Casse-Gueule, origins ringing with military expeditions and daring adventures, they'd been diminished by exile, by bad luck, and by an attenuation of their very name to a grim joke.

Here the narrator's voice is central. He's no mere reporter, he's the interpreter of the world—it's his voice that makes the story comic, lyric, ironic, or mythic.

Effaced narrators make the narration as invisible as possible so that the story seems to be simply telling itself. Readers tend not to think about its particular style, for this mode avoids words and images that draw attention to the narrator:

> Lowell got into the pickup, but didn't start the engine. Before he'd seen the book, it had seemed simple. His daughter was insulted by a boy from town. Lowell knew what had to be done. But the pictures in the book, a sailing-ship in a storm, a knight in armor on his horse looking down at a praying woman, puzzled him. He had to think about this.

An analysis of types of narrators overlaps with the discussion of *point of view*. Certain narrative types are almost certainly also going to be characters within the story. *Naive* narrators are usually characters themselves. You use them when you want to generate satire, irony, or humor. The naive narrator is not necessarily stupid or obtuse. His naïveté may let him make comments that are wiser than those of more sophisticated observers:

> Well, it didn't make sense to me that a Caskit should shoot a Wolf over a Fourth Grade Reader, but everyone else said it was a good idea because once you let someone tromp on your toes, next thing they'll borrow your tractor. So the town was looking forward to a murder and a good long trial, I liked the idea of town being lively for a change, but I wasn't sure if Lisa was going to be happy about Harvey dead, and maybe her daddy too, depending on how the trial went, of course.

Unreliable narrators are untrustworthy characters who try to bend the story for their own reasons:

Caskit was one of those nose-to-the-grindstone types and the Wolfs was show-off do-gooders. If we got lucky someone'd get killed, and the trial would be good for business for a couple of weeks. And on top of that, them families would be done for and the town would belong back to us folks who came here first and deserve it.

Each narrative mode has benefits and costs. *Omniscient* narrators can make observations, but those comments have to be interesting. *Objective* narrators let the story seem to tell itself, but make it hard to get into the characters' minds. *Foregrounded* narrators have lots of freedom, but can easily get in the way of the story itself. *Effaced* narrators create immediacy but have to stay invisible. *Naive* narrators can achieve fine ironies but must stay consistent. *Unreliable* narrators create tension but they're trapped in their own delusions.

Sometimes the narrator tells the story, and sometimes the narrator *is* the story.

See *Facade, Frame Story, Point of View, Style, Voice.*

▼
NATURALISM
⚬ The writers of the naturalist movement in fiction believed that the true nature of men and women was revealed by stripping away the veneer of artificial social structures. Starting in the late nineteenth century, works like Émile Zola's *Germinal,* Stephen Crane's *Maggie: A Girl of the Streets,* Frank Norris's *McTeague,* and Theodore Dreiser's *Sister Carrie* took the novel out of the drawing rooms and into the bedrooms, away from the generals in their tents to the soldiers

in the ditches, to city slums, coal mines, brothels, lifeboats—
wherever life was elemental. That was where you could study
unvarnished human behavior.

The naturalists freed fiction from the prison of middle-class
gentility. They established that poverty, brutality, and violence were valid and necessary subjects for serious fiction.
The lives of opium addicts were as significant as the lives of
princes. You inherit that freedom.

The achievements of naturalism teach valuable lessons. These
writers stressed the value of firsthand experience like Edmond
and Jules de Goncourt, who realized that to write authenti-
cally they had to immerse themselves in their subjects. Naturalists knew that for their fiction to transcend mere sociology
they had to create memorable characters, as in Zola's *Nana*
or James T. Farrell's *Studs Lonigan*. They understood that
psychological or economic forces would remain abstractions
unless they created gripping stories, as in Crane's *The Red
Badge of Courage* or Dreiser's *An American Tragedy*.

Naturalism established the precedent and the rationale for
delving into the darker aspects of human existence. The suffering and the individuality of those who live on the margins
of society were recognized. The naturalists' underlying philosophical principles were a strange mixture of Darwin, Marx,
Freud, and Nietzsche, but they were storytellers first, creating
some of the most vivid scenes and characters in American
literature.

See *Narrative, Profanity/Obscenity, Realism, Sex, Trust Your
Material,* "Write What You Know."

▼
NEGATIVE POSITIVE KNOWLEDGE

◦ This term refers to the technique you use when you want to tell readers what is *not* happening. It addresses the problem of how to call readers' attention to what a character is not saying, or doing, or thinking.

Fiction is silently selective. Readers assume that what you omit is not significant. If you don't mention bathroom behavior, readers assume that the characters' toilet habits have no bearing on the story. Similarly, not commenting on what characters eat or when they do laundry doesn't imply that they are starving or not washing their clothes. If your character's job is described briefly and never mentioned again, readers don't assume that it's making her miserable. They just don't think about it. If you don't tell her childhood memories, describe her bedroom, portray her husband, that signals to readers that these things are not important to know about.

If you do want to draw attention to your character's habit of forgetting about her children for hours at a time, or not eating regularly, or being unable to bring back the image of the room she slept in as a child, you have to create what is not there.

In *The Overcoat* Nikolai Gogol tells what happens "when the gray Petersburg sky is completely overcast and the whole population of clerks has dined and eaten their fill." This single, elaborate sentence goes on for hundreds of words, describing the hours when "all the clerks are scattered about the apartments of their friends, playing a stormy game of whist, sipping tea out of glasses, eating cheap biscuits, sucking smoke from long pipes, telling, as the cards are dealt, some scandal that has floated down from higher levels." And it continues to pile on detail until Gogol closes—"even when everyone was eagerly seeking entertainment, Akaky Akakievich did not indulge in any amusement." We vividly feel Akaky's isolation by our knowing the rich world that Akaky is *not* experiencing.

You can tell what a character is not understanding. In fiction it feels like no violation of point of view to have a phrase like:

> Patrick stared at Helen and she looked back hard. He refused to think about what might happen next.

Don't be afraid of saying what your character doesn't know, is forgetting, repressing, or avoiding. If he's puzzled, show that.

> Patrick thought Helen just plain fell out of love with him— no reason at all. But he couldn't be sure. That last fight was so ferocious—you don't throw a fish at someone you don't care about. But he didn't understand what he had done. What drove her crazy like that?

See *Exposition, Sex.*

▼

NOVEL

○ The novel seems to be just about anything written in prose that claims to be fictional and is long enough to be considered a book.

Exceptions test even that definition. Chaucer's long narrative poem *Troilus and Criseyde* is often discussed as a novel.

Max Ernst subtitled *Une Semaine de Bonté* (*A Week of Kindness*), a wordless series of approximately two hundred engraved pictures, "a novel." Julian Barnes's critical essay *Flaubert's Parrot* is a brilliant novel.

Novels vary drastically in length, in structure, in scope, and in content. They have been written in the form of letters, diaries, dreams, visions, memoirs, monologues, confessions, collages, poems, and commentaries on poems. They have been written entirely in dialogue and entirely without dialogue. They have ranged from fragmented little observations of tiny moments to encyclopedic epics embracing entire cultures. They have been written with multiple endings so readers can choose the one that pleases most, and they have been written on loose pages so that readers can continually rearrange the entire narrative.

The novel is an odd form in other ways, too. Most works of art are experienced in a single viewing, or in an evening. But most novels demand days or weeks of time. Reading itself is a demanding activity. So writers of novels have to give their audience urgent reasons to keep on reading.

Whatever form you work in, from the most traditional to the most experimental, all writers have the same problem: how to get readers to keep turning pages. The longer and the more demanding the book, the more acute the problem becomes. What is going to impel your readers forward? Accuracy can be admired, but it doesn't generate momentum. True wisdom is valuable, but it doesn't create a desperate need to know what happens next. Verbal ingenuity can be appreciated but it can also cause fatigue. A well-written page is a beautiful thing, but it alone is not gasoline.

Hundreds of studies of the novel have been written and this

book can't begin to cover all that need be said. Part IV, "Readables," lists some useful works, and those books mention many more books. John Gardner's *On Becoming a Novelist* is a good place to start.

See *Character, Cliff-hanger, Freytag's Pyramid, Narrator, Plot,* "Readables," *Suspense, Tension.*

▼

OBJECTIVE CORRELATIVE

T. S. Eliot defined this term as the use of the specific and concrete to express abstract ideas in literature. As he put it, you need "a set of objects, a situation, a chain of events" to create a "sensory experience" so that "the emotion is immediately invoked." The concept has always been controversial. First of all, Eliot summoned it to explain why *Hamlet* was an "artistic failure." Second, critics have been in constant disagreement as to its meaning.

Even with that confusion, the objective correlative can still be useful to writers of fiction. Ideas and feelings are more vivid if they are expressed by a powerful, palpable image. When we remember works of fiction, we recall objects and actions, not thoughts and abstractions. In Ken Kesey's *One Flew Over the Cuckoo's Nest* modern society is embodied by the insane asylum. The titles of Hawthorne's *The Scarlet Letter*, Kafka's *The Trial*, Katherine Anne Porter's *Ship of Fools*, Walker Percy's *The Moviegoer*, or Ralph Ellison's *Invisible Man* suggest the objective correlatives that unify each work.

See *Imagery, Metaphor and Simile, Motif, Symbolism.*

▼

PARABLE

○   A parable is a very short tale that often carries a moral or spiritual message.

Unlike fables, which usually append a moral to make sure everyone gets the point, parables are often cryptic. Unlike allegories, which may be puzzling at first but have a code that, once understood, makes clear what everything means, parables do not have a clear relationship between the story and the interpretation. Biblical parables, the most famous of which are the parables of Jesus, tell of mustard seeds and bridesmaids; they dramatize subtle religious questions, but they often have several possible interpretations.

Contemporary parables are not easy to create. Would-be parable makers tend to fall into hokey oracular cadences or some other highly mannered style. Since parables are both mysterious and meaningful, they can sound confused and portentous. Writers of parables often neglect the first necessity—to tell a good story well. But parables remain fascinating because of the tension between a brief anecdote and the elusive evocation of philosophical and spiritual mysteries. Shirley Jackson's "The Lottery" develops the idea of the parable into a classic short story that admits of no single interpretation, and so remains forever open to new meanings.

See *Allegory, Didacticism, Satire, Style.*

▼

PARODY

○   Parody is an imitation of a literary work or style that exaggerates and caricatures the features of the original. Parodies might have serious satirical intent in mocking affectations or pretentions. Mark Twain's "Story of the Little Bad Boy" expresses his annoyance at the falsity of didactic children's fiction. Ernest Hemingway's *Torrents of Spring* was a serious, personal assault on Sherwood Anderson's prose style (a style that had greatly influenced Hemingway). Or parodies might simply be humorous, like Robert Benchley's stories from Greek mythology about Polygaminous, the God of Ensilage, and Endocrine, the Goddess of Lettuce.

Literary criticism has attempted to distinguish between varieties of parodies with terms like *burlesque* (characterized by exaggeration of a literary form rather than a particular work), *travesty* (a serious subject made to look silly), and *mock epic* (a silly subject treated as if it were terribly serious), but the more you look at the definitions the more tangled they get. If you burlesque a form (the Western), you might also parody particular works (*High Noon*), and one scene might be travesty (hero and villain assailed by hiccups during gun battle) and another part might be mock heroic (awesome tension over who can blow larger bubble-gum bubble).

Parody is a perilous form. You have to be a literary comic-impressionist, able to select salient characteristics of the original work so that your readers recognize it in a new way. The work you are parodying needs to be admired or fashionable enough to make the assault worthwhile. Once readers get the joke, the parody has to stay interesting. Nathanael West's *A Cool Million* succeeds by turning his parody of Horatio Alger novels into a critique of American society. In the last few years writers with distinctive styles, like Hemingway, Faulkner, and Bulwer-Lytton, have been the subjects of highly publicized literary parody contests.

See *Comedy, Farce, Satire.*

▼

PATHETIC FALLACY

o   John Ruskin coined this term to express his disapproval of phrases that gave passions and conscious intentions to natural phenomena, such as "the gay leaves danced merrily," or "a vengeful wind tortured the cringing flowers." They're "fallacies" because the images are so often corny, clichéd, or strained: "The evening said its prayers as the sun sank gratefully in her watery bed." Pathetic fallacies don't have to be about nature: "The doorknob greeted his hand."

Some writers who have been told about the pathetic fallacy worry about it too much. "Pathetic fallacy!" they shout in dismay, as if they've spotted a fly in their soup.

Actually, good writers often use such imagery. James Dickey looks at tin cans in the mud, "their lids pried-up and cruel," or notes a swift river's "alertness and resourcefulness" as it sweeps over stones and rocks. Metaphors frequently ascribe impossible feelings to nature and natural objects. If you keep using literalist similes ("it was as if," "it was like," "it appeared that") you'll just clutter your prose. A style that attributes feelings to the inanimate world can create strong effects and fresh perceptions. The real principle is this: If it works, it's called a lively metaphor—if it doesn't, it's a pathetic fallacy.

See *Cliché, Metaphor and Simile.*

▼

PICARO

o   A picaro (from the Spanish *pícaro*, meaning rogue) is a lively rascal who gets into adventures that reveal the folly or vices of other, ostensibly more respectable characters. The anonymous Spanish work *Lazarillo de Tormes* (1554), the first picaresque novel, began an enthusiasm that spread to other countries, but the masterpiece of the form is Cervantes' *Don Quixote*.

Picaresque novels are usually composed of loosely connected escapades. Despite his ephemeral successes and brushes with disaster, the personality of the picaro usually remains unchanged. In some picaresque novels episodes are linked by the reappearance of previously introduced characters. The plot can be given direction if the picaro has a quest or goal.

The form is still popular. It's a way of placing an unconventional, somewhat disreputable hero at the center of your work, getting him involved in an interesting adventure, and then moving him on to another adventure. If you want your readers to identify with your character, you need to keep him engaging despite his vices. Keep his crimes petty, his success ephemeral, and his victims unattractive. The picaro can reveal the inadequacies of a society that is more corrupt than he is. Mark Twain's *Huckleberry Finn*, Jack Kerouac's *On the Road*, Saul Bellow's *The Adventures of Augie March*, and Tom Robbins's *Even Cowgirls Get the Blues* have all done variations on the picaresque. Women picaros are part of the tradition, from Daniel Defoe's *Moll Flanders* to Erica Jong's dauntless Isadora Wing in *Fear of Flying*.

See *Anti-hero, Character*.

▼

PLACES AND PLACE NAMES

○ If your stories take place in Patagonia or Mongolia, you have your readers' attention from the start. Graham Greene knew that, and so do Paul Theroux and

V. S. Naipaul. So did Homer. The allure of the exotic seems timeless. The writer is returning from a foreign land with wondrous tales.

This doesn't mean that far away is "better." Few writers have been raised in Uttar Pradesh. If the Jericho you're from is on Long Island and your Naples is in Florida, you need to recognize the strangeness and exoticism of those places, too. They have their own odd customs, sinister rituals, sights and smells. Places you know are not necessarily familiar to others. You can create Atlanta and Altoona with the same energy, the same attention to detail, the same sensuousness, as Somerset Maugham gave to Malaya, Peking, and Samoa.

When you place your fiction in world-famous locations like Los Angeles or Paris or Harvard University, you establish geographical authenticity. Your readers already have an image of Hollywood, or the Eiffel Tower, or an ivy-league college quadrangle. You can be fairly sure that settings like the Watts Towers or the Louvre or Brattle Street conjure up some image for many of your readers. But don't rely on that familiarity to do your work for you. You still have to create the place on the page. Name-dropping of boulevards and parks won't substitute for real description. There's another pitfall, too. Real places commit you to their real layout. You can't put a cathedral across the street from New York's Metropolitan Museum of Art, even if your plot desperately needs one there.

Walker Percy wanted to set *Lancelot* in New Orleans, but he also wanted to alter its geography for his own purposes. He explains his solution in his headnote: "Though the setting of this novel appears to be New Orleans and the River Road, this city and this famous road are used here as place names of an imaginary terrain." Percy's work is intensely involved with a specific place, yet he cleverly retains his artistic freedom.

Another strategy is to make up a place name—Costa Piñata, Pennzburgh, or Elihu University. The knowledgeable reader has a sense of the real place behind the pseudonym, but you're free to install your own library, put the river near the train station, and rewrite history.

Place situates the story in your reader's mind. Fiction that seems to happen in no particular place often seems not to take place at all.

See *Accuracy, Description, Names, Trust Your Material,* "Write What You Know."

▼

PLOT

○ Plot means the story line. When people talk about plotting, they usually mean how to set up the situation, where to put the turning points, and what the characters will be doing in the end. In brief, they are talking about *what happens.* Plotting concerns how to move characters in and out of your story. Plotting means what you do to keep the action going. For example, in detective fiction the classic rule is that when the action slows down, have someone come in the room with a gun. (Metaphorically speaking, that's not bad advice for any writer.)

In a good plot, cause and effect interlink. Each situation sets up the next situation. For example:

> Arthur Garble moves into a new house with his ferocious-looking but gentle pit bull. The dog makes his neighbors nervous and so they are unfriendly. That upsets Arthur,

and he is rude to them. Their reaction is to persecute him. Some neighbors, however, take his side. Soon people are arguing wherever they meet. After a particularly heated interchange, they realize they have lost control of themselves while the controversial dog has remained peaceful and serene.

Misunderstanding begot unfriendliness; unfriendliness nurtured hostility; hostility led to anger; anger turned into confrontation; confrontation precipitated recognition; and recognition brought about reconciliation. The plot doesn't go off on a tangent by turning into a love story. The plot doesn't violate its premises by bringing in some outside factor (*deus ex machina*) in the end—such as having the dog save a child from a burning building. Its resolution lies in its characters and the situation.

The shorter the piece of fiction, the less need for plot. You can write a fine story in which little happens: A man curses his neighbor, a widow quits her mah-jongg group, or an unhappy family goes on a picnic. Simple shapes work better than something fussy and complicated.

In novels, plot seems more important. I say *seems* because the concept of plot confuses writers. They'll say, "I want to write, but I can't think of good plots." They are worrying about the wrong thing. Though they do have to create an interesting story line, it doesn't have to be complicated—it doesn't have to be plotty. "The Shapes of Fiction," Part I of this book, explains the basic building blocks of fiction. In novels these shapes get extended, combined, and multiplied. The *Journey* becomes Charlotte Brontë's *Jane Eyre*. The *Visitation* precipitates the plot of Emily Brontë's *Wuthering Heights*.

A plot can, like a journey, begin with a single step. A woman making up her mind to recover her father's oil paintings may be enough to start. The journey begins there, as it did for Raskolnikov in *Crime and Punishment* when he decided to commit his crime. You might even say that every novel is a quest novel. The characters will be seeking freedom or truth, revenge or exoneration, peace or sanity. They're searching for their fathers or mothers or their roots. True love or salvation. Or money, marriage, and success. Or themselves. Read Tobias Smollett or Henry Fielding, Lore Segal or Anne Tyler— everybody's looking for something.

The plot grows out of what helps and what hinders the characters' progress toward their goals. Some beginning plot elements might go like this:

> Andy Giannino is a kid who wants to be let alone. He's looking forward to a free summer with plenty of reading. But Andy's parents send him off to a military summer camp. He's miserable until the nature counselor befriends him and gets him to make meticulous drawings of insect larvae. On visiting day Andy's father is furious thinking that Andy is not learning to become manly. Andy's mother thinks the drawings look disgusting. They take him home at once. Andy starts hanging around with a guy known only as Goofer. Goofer reads during the day and buys stolen property at night. Goofer shows Andy how to steal copper from power plants. [And so on.]

Andy Giannino's quest is for survival and for self-knowledge. The other characters have their own quests. The father is trying to improve himself by listening nightly to motivational tapes. The mother is trying to make the family fit an ideal American stereotype because, she believes, then she will be happy. The rhythms of their advances and setbacks develop the story.

When poorly conceived, plot creates problems. An over-complicated plot can make a book seem contrived or confusing. A lack of plot can make a book seem meandering or static. But plot alone can't make a fiction vital, witty, moving, informative, or wise. That comes from character, dialogue, description, and narrative style.

When we call a novel plotless we mean that the writer has not created that interlinking of cause and effect—has not deployed intrigants, developed momentum, or used the traditional narrative devices that seduce and impel readers through the work. (The picaresque novel has often been called plotless, though the opposite seems true—it's made up of a great many separate plots.) Novelists who eschew plot have captivated readers by their delicious prose, profound meditations, intense visions, and political insights, but the longer the work, the harder it is to keep readers' attention all the way to the end.

See *Character, Cliff-hanger, Freytag's Pyramid, Intrigant, Narrative, Novel, Position, Premise, Tension, Zigzag.*

▼

POETIC JUSTICE

○ Poetic justice implies that the characters in the story get what they deserve.

In tragedy, poetic justice can mean that admirable figures may die, but they'll be ennobled in their downfall, while the wicked will die in disgrace. In comedy, the good finally get their wishes granted, and the bad are embarrassed into repentance for their vices. Those endings are appropriate for each genre. Poetic justice will, however, seem heavy-handed when it's used simplistically to give a story a sentimental ending. The hero gets the girl and the ranch; the villain gets burned up in the fire he set. It's hard to take that kind of juridical symmetry seriously.

But poetic justice can refer to much more subtle resolutions. Faulkner's *The Sound and the Fury* and Ellison's *Invisible Man* leave the characters neither rewarded nor punished in any definite way, but the endings are aesthetically satisfying, poetically just.

See *Endings, Irony, Resolution.*

▼

POINT OF VIEW

○ This refers to the central consciousness that narrates the tale. The usual classification is pronominal—point of view is first, second, or third person. But that's just the beginning.

○○ *First-person point of view* ○○

First person allows you to engage in one of the most natural of human social activities. "Last night," you begin, "the strangest thing happened to me as I was walking by the pond." First person is immediate, engaging, and instantly convincing. You create a distinctive voice, a character, a personality, with the first words of the story. Your readers want to know what happens next. And first person itself has a range of possibilities.

The most immediate first-person voice creates a story that seems to be happening as the voice tells it:

> I unscrewed the lid. I looked inside. It looked green and gooey. I stuck my finger in it. Yucch!

Present tense emphasizes immediacy even more:

> I open the door. The room is black. I feel something hot and wet pushing into my ear.

But first person can also achieve great distance:

> It was almost sixty years ago. My four grandparents were still alive, and they would pass me around to comment on my inadequacies. My nose was the chief offense.

The time spectrum has infinite gradations. The story that is told as if it is happening at that moment is told by a first-person narrator—an *I*—that is a single character. The story that is told at some remove from the event implies two *I*'s: the person who experienced the anecdote when it happened some time ago and the person who now tells the story. That second *I* can be relatively transparent. Though readers are aware that the events took place in the past, there is no particular emphasis on the situation of the present *I* who is telling the story. Or the first-person narrator might call attention to herself, point out how time and experience have made her who she is, who she was, and reflect on the relationship between past and present. The story might even be as much about the difficulties of recalling the past, or the way feelings and understanding change, as it is about the long-ago event itself.

Not only can you choose how long ago the story might have happened to the narrator, but you can also choose how accurate or how distorted the narrator's version of events is going to be. On the one hand, there is the *I* readers are invited to accept as the voice of true perceptions, accurate observations, sound judgments, and admirable feelings. Way out on the other hand, there is the *I* who is insane, unaware that his vision of the world and of other people is drastically warped. In between are the *I*'s who are fallible or mendacious in different ways and to various degrees—an *I* who doesn't realize he is stubborn or naive or self-absorbed or an *I* we can see is lying to himself or the readers.

How central should the first-person narrator be to the story? There are many possibilities. The simplest form is the *I* telling a story about himself:

> I looked directly into the catamount's eyes. I knew it was him or me.

Then there is the story whose apparent subject is another person or other people:

> Who I most remember from those days was John Trespas and his crowd—wild, doomed, and coruscating with an energy that the community hated.

In between are the *I*'s who tell about themselves and others with varying degrees of intimacy:

> I'd walk home with Ozzie after a den meeting and we'd plan weird stuff to do to the other Cubs. I think there was something wrong with both of us.

Remember that the first-person narrator, as the voice of the story, is necessarily part of the story. The *I* must be as important as any other major character. Otherwise the *I* is an extra person. Your readers will wonder why he is hanging around if he has nothing to do but narrate—they'll think, why don't you tell the story and let the *I* go home?

The difficulties of first-person narration are directly related to its advantages. The first-person narrator, so convincing because of that confiding voice, needs to stay within character. The voice—the vocabulary, speech rhythms, imagery, and insights—must add up to a person we believe in. If readers believe, they will believe in the world that person describes.

But if the voice sometimes sounds like a character,

> —So I look in the window and there's this fat guy with a cigar bent over one of those little hot-dog-type dogs, and, it looks like he's trying to get it to smoke his damn cheroot—

and sometimes sounds like an author,

> —It was a strange scene. Human and canine wreathed in gray smoke, the man offering his beloved tobacco, for what reason? love? loneliness? a joke born of despair?—

and sometimes sounds like no one in particular,

> —I left and walked down the street because it was getting dark and I still had a few errands to run before dinner.

the story falls apart.

The *I* is the only voice your readers can hear directly in

first-person narration. Everything and everybody must be filtered through this voice. Other characters are known only through the first-person point of view. So if you want to give intimate knowledge of other characters' thoughts and emotions, you have to find another way. The first-person narrator can have insights appropriate to the point of view, but it may be necessary for your other characters to reveal themselves, either in their own words or in what they say about each other.

A first-person narrative has to find a way of letting its readers see the narrator. *I* tells us nothing about name, age, sex, shape, or color. People actually do think a lot about what they look like, not only when they stare in a mirror (a device that has become a cliché) or when they look at photographs or pictures in magazines, but also when they compare themselves, for better or worse, to people they know or meet. You need to bring in people for the *I* to interact with and to create vivid physical actions or the story becomes internal and static as the *I* thinks and thinks, and readers feel as if everything is taking place in the *I*'s head.

Writers can have problems in getting information to their first-person narrator. They're driven to improbable eavesdropping or inadvertent private-letter reading. Coincidences are contrived. Coincidences, however, are a tricky business. When set up carefully, there can be a psychological inevitability that readers accept. Set up carelessly, they seem a cheap way of handling plot. The difference between success and failure lies not in the coincidence, but in the preparation.

If the *I* is unreliable, you must find ways of making that evident in the story. You have to embed such things as contradictions, exaggerations, other voices, or different versions of reality so that the *I*'s distortions can be discerned and understood by your readers. The classics of the demented *I* come from Edgar Allan Poe—"Berenice" or "The Cask of Amontillado." The narrators' feverish voices signal their emotional disturbance. In Ford Madox Ford's *The Good Soldier,* the narrator is so pedantically precise that we rightly suspect there's something seriously wrong with him.

A minor consequence of first-person narration ought to be mentioned. Except for rather odd stories, we know that the first person survived long enough to write (or think about or tell) this narrative. So suspense is moderated by certainty.

Memorable fiction has been written in first person. Ishmael in Melville's *Moby-Dick,* Huck in Twain's *The Adventures of Huckleberry Finn,* Jake Barnes in Hemingway's *The Sun Also Rises,* and Holden Caulfield in Salinger's *The Catcher in the Rye* are among the important first-person characters in American literature.

Many first-person narrations are in the form of a memoir or diary or series of letters. But in the United States, the spoken voice has become the predominant medium by which the story is told. There's a naturalness to the spoken first-person narration that expresses the freshness and vitality of American speech. First person is your most subtle, supple, and valuable literary resource.

∘∘ *Second-person point of view* ∘∘

Writers like to experiment with second person. There's an appealing quality to addressing your readers and overtly making them part of your story:

> You stood over the bed. You looked sorrowfully at the sleeping cat, the sleeping dog, the sleeping man.

There are a variety of second-person possibilities. One is really a displacement for first person. You might feel that *I* sounds too egotistical or too confining. When a lyric poet says *I*—as in "I fall upon the thorns of life! I bleed!"—readers take that to mean the poet, not a character created by the poet. *You* can have intimacy as *I* does, but also be somewhat disassociated from *I*. With *You*, the ego of the story moves off center a bit:

> You can't think, can't write, can't call her up. You do any-
> way. "How's it going?" you say. She says, "Well, well, well,
> what have we here?"

Another sort of second person is in fact a more egotistical form of *I*, actually an intensification of the *I*—this is the detective story *I*:

> You go down the street. You smell the city. You can't stand
> the stench, the lies, the reek of corruption. But you have to.
> It's your job. You're a cop.

The *I* here is so big it can't contain itself in one person and demands that it be *You* too.

Second person also helps you achieve a relatively disembodied tone—a creation of a *You* that implies every person and addresses a widely shared condition or feeling:

> It's two days before Christmas and you still haven't bought
> the right gifts and you're frantic. What can you find now?

Or second person can be used in quite a different way. You invite your readers to be somebody they clearly are not. *You* puts them inside a character and asks them to experience the world through that character:

> You feel the stick in your back. "Move on buddy." You move on, keeping your face down. Looking up means you're looking for trouble.

The use of present tense often seems right for second person, but past or future is just as possible.

Second-person narration is striking and powerful, but it can feel insistent and aggressive. It demands that your readers *be* someone instead of merely observing someone. It can feel fresh, or it can seem tiresome, affected, or merely modish.

Its possibilities are perhaps just beginning to be explored.

∘∘ *Third-person point of view* ∘∘

Third-person storytelling is an ancient literary strategy. It's the natural mode when telling about someone else's adventures. So if you are speaking of the life of a hero of the tribe or of the misfortunes of a friend or what befell an aunt, it seems but part of our language to use that person's name and to refer to her in the third person.

The use of the third person presents you with a number of decisions. First, should the story be told as if it's through the eyes and in the mind of only one person? This method, in which the point of view is limited to one person and one consciousness, is close to the feeling of first-person point of view. To compare:

> I just jammed clothes in the suitcase without looking. It was crazy. I was cramming in shirts I never wore and fist-

fuls of ties and dress handkerchiefs. I hated Jack. I hated Sis. I wanted to get out of the house as soon as possible.

Scooper jammed his clothes in the suitcase without looking. He felt crazy. He crammed in shirts he never wore and fistfuls of ties and dress handkerchiefs. He hated Jack. He hated Sis. He wanted to get out of the house as soon as possible.

In the second example, the narrator is almost invisible. Readers experience the story through Scooper's mind. Third person used in this way allows the immediacy of first person, but the separate voice of the narrator allows some flexibility. You aren't entirely limited to the perceptions, knowledge, and vocabulary of the character:

Scooper drove down Druidic Drive and on to Whispering Way, not thinking about where he was going or what he was going to do. He didn't want to think about whether he had money in his wallet or to see if he had gas in the tank. What he wanted to do was drive, recklessly, endlessly, and somehow, simultaneously, have everyone around him admit to their misperceptions, their callousness, their insensitivity, to say stop, we're sorry, it's our fault, we understand you.

Third person does not have to be limited to one person. Individual sections of stories and novels can be told from other points of view—from inside the heads of different characters. So the next section might start:

Jane stared out of the picture window. Just like Scooper, she thought. Just like him not to understand what he did to

me, to Jack, or what he's doing to himself. She rubbed her
thumb against the wet window until it squeaked.

One thing remains constant here: Whichever character's point
of view is being used, that's how the readers must see the
world for that section. The narrator remains for the most
part invisible. The writer wants us to stay within the characters' minds as much as possible.

The concentrated energy of a short story makes third-person limited consciousness an effective point of view. Henry
James is credited with seeing its possibilities for creating complicated psychological portraits and for dramatizing how variously characters perceive reality. But you don't have to adhere
to a single consciousness (or limit yourself to consciousness
serial monogamy). It's possible to have a teller of a story who
says what various characters, major and minor, are thinking,
without line breaks, section breaks, or separate chapters. Such
a narrator is somewhat more visible than our first variety. For
example:

> Scooper and Jane stared at the toaster. This was the morn-
> ing toast fight. If Scooper could just get Jane to leave it
> alone, it would get properly crunchy. Jane pretended there
> was something out the window. Scooper turned his head
> with hers. She reached out and popped the slide up. Jane
> knew he couldn't say anything now. It was perfect—a lovely
> light yellow. She smiled. "Hey Scooper, want me to butter
> one for you?"

Once you establish that you will have access to the thoughts
of more than one character, you can move into other points
of view even in casual encounters:

Jane asked sweetly, "Mr. Berbard, how much are the pork chops today?"

"For you, $4.50 apiece." The man had learned years ago that the price didn't really matter—these were well-to-do people. The *for you* mattered, as if they had an insatiable hunger to be connected, even to the butcher they barely saw.

"Wrap up eight," Jane said. "Nice ones."

Or you can be more overt, giving access to the thoughts and feelings of a number of your characters in a single story, taking on the responsibility of the psychologist, sociologist, historian, and storyteller. Magically, you know the characters better than they know each other and better than they know themselves. You might comment on the social customs of the period, make generalizations about behavior in the culture, and speculate on causes. Readers may come to understand the lives of those within the fiction better than they know the lives of those they live with:

Granger Nearfoy was a respected man. His neighbors came to him with their cracked harrows, their problems with tomatoes, and, late at night, their broken hearts. Tossich, who grew strawberries, came one evening. In the manner of the time, they never looked each other in the eye. For serious discussion men stared at the fire, the words would hang in the darkness, and they could keep their dignity while revealing their deepest failures. Granger had heard many things, and often the things he heard had no solution—they only meant more sorrow. He gave Tossich a tumbler of brandy. Tossich turned the tumbler in his hand. He was not accustomed to asking for help, and this was shameful to him—he was still young, he was strong. He thought about telling of some lesser problem . . .

You might even emphasize your God-like power as a creator and manipulator of your characters and explicitly refer to them as creations, toys, puppets, or actors. When books make reference to the omniscient narrator, they usually mean something of this sort:

> So perhaps you have heard enough of our friend Tossich and his problems, so grand to him and so minuscule (pardon me) to the reader. And so let us send him home in his Dodge Mini-van. Let us perhaps take a gander (pardon me again) at Tossich's rosy wife, Anna, who is now in close conversation with a person who has not yet been introduced. Robert Smythe is charming and energetic. He speaks movingly of his sad childhood and eloquently of his hopes for a little happiness. He is one of the most beguiling sociopaths one could ever hope to meet—as hollow and dead inside as he is sympathetic and warm outside—and Tossich's wife has fallen for him like a bale of hay.

The word *omniscient*, however, is not totally accurate, for even here you can vary your degree of omniscience, apparently having access to certain characters' motivations but not to others, warning readers of some dangers but remaining unaware of others, and making other disclaimers revealing your lack of total knowledge.

> It is said that Granger sent Smythe a letter. No one knew what it said, but soon after, Smythe mysteriously disappeared. Since then, every summer Tossich sends Granger a tray of red strawberries.

These various possibilities within third-person point of view lead to different types of stories.

Writers who limit themselves to a single third-person point of view can create a character whose understanding of the world may be the very subject of the story. Your readers live through the character's mind and feel as the character does. And yet, since the narrative is in third person, you can draw on an authorial voice not strictly limited to the vocabulary or perceptions of the character. The advantages are the creation of immediacy, intimacy, and psychological depth, while retaining the freedom to continue to be a narrator outside of the central character. This is a mode particularly suited to the short story because of its intensity, its concentration, and its possibility for plunging readers very quickly into a character's situation.

Its problems are that readers basically get one character's version of reality. Sometimes you, as writer, identify more closely with the character than your readers are willing to. You may believe your character is sympathetic and sensitive, but readers find him self-centered and stupid. Another problem is making the other characters vivid. Since the narrative point of view is also the main character, that voice and presence have center stage. You have to have enough stories within your story, including talk and action from other characters, in order for those characters to have real presence too.

When you have several points of view some problems are solved. You have the intimacy of individual points of view, and the narrative is freed from the limitations of the single character. At the same time other problems are created. You must bring to life a variety of people, convincingly and interestingly, who reveal either your uncanny imagination or, on a bad day, your inadequate empathy. Unless you develop a distinctive voice for each point of view, your characters will all sound alike.

The omniscient narrator has the opportunity to comment in his own voice, to introduce historical information, to philosophize about human behavior, and to make insightful remarks about his characters' behavior. This is a burden that some gladly bear, and others find oppressive. It is a claim to authority that must be managed with grace and wit.

∘∘ *Choosing points of view* ∘∘

Selecting the best point of view from which to tell a story can be puzzling. Because you originally conceive a story in first or third person doesn't mean it has to stay that way. Often it's good to rewrite the story in another person to see how it changes. Sometimes writers, after a number of drafts, have realized that the real story lies elsewhere—in the mother's view of the daughter, not the daughter's view of the mother. Such changes in perspective have resulted in breakthroughs that have astonished their own authors.

To sum up, first person is tricky, because it seems easy at the beginning but presents all sorts of traps as you go on. Second person is dramatic but strained. Third person focused through a single character combines intimacy and flexibility, but the relationship between narrator and character can be troublesome. Third person with a different viewpoint in each section allows a richness of characterization, but the separate parts must create a unified work. Third person through a variably omniscient narrator means that the voice has to be charming or witty or intellectually strong enough to command respect.

Find the point of view that seems comfortable for you. If your strength lies in your gift for "doing voices"—you feel natural thinking as a grandmother, a small child, or an irritated mechanic—then it makes sense to write from those points of view. If you tend toward quirky imagery and a distinctive style that result in your characters sounding like each other, let one voice unify the story and create your world.

See *Character, Flashback, Interior Monologue, Narrator, Psychic Distance, Stream of Consciousness.*

▼
POSITION

○ This is not a traditional literary term, but it gives you a useful way to think about character and plot. Your character's *position* in the work at any time is a complex of internal and external factors. His internal position means, for example, what he knows and how he feels. His external position means his relationship to other people and to social institutions, such as his marriage or job.

For example, your character is Derwig, a depressed, anxious, twenty-eight-year-old man. Derwig is unmarried and lonely; he is a kitchen appliance salesman and a heavy drinker. That complex of internal and external forces makes up your character's position.

Once readers understand a character's position, they're waiting to see that position change. Since we know Derwig is a lonely kitchen appliance salesman and a heavy drinker, having him careen from bar to bar may change his level of intoxication, but it might not change his position. Whatever happens to Derwig, whatever situations he's in—rude to the bartender, argumentative with other customers, kicked out of the bar, staggering back to his apartment to find some more beer in the fridge—he is still a lonely guy and a heavy drinker. In a certain way, though interesting events have taken place, nothing has happened in the story. His position has been demonstrated and dramatized through various situations, but it remains basically the same.

Now if Derwig gets a phone call at the apartment and is told that he's fired, that is a change in his position. He's now an unemployed lonely guy and a heavy drinker. Readers feel something has happened. As they learn that Derwig has about eighty dollars in his checking account, that he will not be able to cover his rent which is due in a week, and that he doesn't have friends or relatives to help him, they understand more about his position, but that position doesn't change until he gets a salesman's job on a used-car lot. It changes again when he realizes it is a chop shop dealing in stolen parts and reconstituted vehicles.

Position is a concept that helps you understand plot. It helps you understand why some novels can have a lot of incident but move slowly and seem flat, while other novels move quickly and keep readers' interest high. Plot and position work together. Plot is the mechanism that changes your character's position.

You control the pace of the story by the rate at which you change the positions of the characters. A story in which positions change every few pages moves rapidly. The rate of change makes stories accelerate or decelerate. This control allows you to create a structural rhythm for the narrative as a whole.

Derwig's rise in the stolen-car business changes his position. He meets people. He gains confidence. He gives up drinking. A young woman who owns a donut 'n' coffee truck is attracted to him. He starts to make deals on his own. His position keeps changing. Then Derwig gets a tip that the police are watching the business.

Readers see changes in position as either good or bad for the character. But once readers see a trend—all is now going well for Derwig—they redefine Derwig's position as *improving*. That might put him into interesting situations but readers won't feel a drastic change until something threatens him. Then he might be put in new positions, as a threatened man, a chased man, a man on the run. Readers tend to be impatient. They look forward to changes of position, especially when the reverses of good and bad fortune occur rapidly. The faster the changes occur, the more tension is created.

Suspense novels devote themselves to these sensations to the exclusion of almost everything else. You'll hear people say, "It's great. Really exciting. The plot's so convoluted you can't understand it but it doesn't make any difference." This might be fine for suspense fiction, but serious novels also need movement, plot, and a continual dynamic of situations and positions. Serious novels are more subtle. The changes in these novels might have to do with growing awarenesses and changing relationships rather than car chases and triple agents, but they're based on the same structural principles. In Henry James's *The Ambassadors* the central character doesn't do much more than talk, listen, watch, and think. But his position is constantly changing. Each new observation, each new idea, puts him closer to or further from his goal.

Your character's position may change in short fiction, too. But it isn't as crucial as it is in a novel. Many short stories are explorations, not transformations, of character. You can write a story about a situation or a moment, and render it so that you give your readers insight into a network of tensions. The movement in a story might not take your character from position A to position B but, inward, from surface to depth. Your readers move to an understanding, an enlightenment. The scale of a novel, however, demands significant movement right from the start. As soon as readers understand the positions of the various characters, they want to see those positions begin to change. That's when the book starts happening.

See *Character, Epiphany, Plot, Suspense, Tension, Zigzag.*

▼
PREMISE
:
○   The premises of a story are what readers accept on faith in order for the story to begin.

Readers are willing to believe in the world you present even if it violates their sense of reality. So a story may start:

> In a small village in Romania there is a family of three-eyed gypsies. They never travel, for in the past they have been viciously persecuted and even killed by the fearful, ignorant peasants of the region.

The more assuredly you establish the premise, the more inclined your readers are to believe it and to enter your world with curiosity. You can tell them that it is A.D. 3000 and the world is run by penguins. You can tell them it is 30,000 B.C. and humans and animals speak freely with one another, often arguing about the meaning of life. Readers are willing to say, "All right. I believe it. So tell me the story."

More prosaic premises still need to be established with authority. A story can be based on the premise that a married woman has an affair with a minister or on the premise that a restless young man signs up for a job on a whaling ship with a strange crew. The premise is the germ from which the story grows.

There is also a premise in the choice of literary genre. A story that presents itself as a realistic depiction of a single mother trying to raise her talented son in a bigoted rural town violates its realistic premises if it resolves its problems by revealing at the end that the child is the secret clone of the violinist Yehudi Menuhin.

There is also the premise of the narrator. If your narrator starts

> Marika and Joven hated each other with the delicious hate
> of tart lemonade,

you've implicitly established an omniscient narrator who might tell what Marika and Joven are thinking and who will comment on them freely. Whatever the narrative voice, the prose style you choose to start with—whether colloquial, lyrical, learned, or neutral—is part of the stylistic premise of the story. Or if you start with alternating voices, that's another kind of premise.

You can change premises, but it's risky business. If you add new premises, ones that do not grow out of the original premise, readers become suspicious.

There's no clear rule to separate a story that's delightfully imaginative from one that is merely unbelievable. There's no clear rule, except that what works, works. You can make readers fetch, but not too far.

See *Beginnings, Narrator, Suspension of Disbelief.*

▼

PROFANITY / OBSCENITY

○ Characters can be a rowdy bunch—cursing, blaspheming, talking rude and crude. If you're writing about such people, you need to render that speech convincingly. For certain groups expletives and strong language have little emotional weight—they're used to add emphasis, rhythm, and flavor to speech, but they don't necessarily signal intense emotions. Some people can't utter a sentence, and sometimes can't get through a single word ("absofuckinglutely"), without an expletive. There's even a kind of affection expressed through obscenity, a bonding created by the violation of the ordinary laws of polite conversation. It's a form of intimacy, private as opposed to public speech.

Even so, a little obscenity in a story goes a long way. Offensive language seems much heavier on paper than it does in the air. Repetition quickly gets rank. To avoid that, use the same principles as for dialect. You're *suggesting* a style of talking, not making a recording. You're creating characters through their language. If they're poetically obscene, the poetry has to be apparent. If their profanity is affectionate, that has to be felt.

Used too frequently, blasphemy and profanity will overshadow the character. But even worse is to be squeamish and euphemistic. "Jumpin' Jehoshaphat, that blankety-blank son of a parsnip stole my Gol-dern car" sounds false and corny. If you aren't comfortable writing about foul-mouthed characters, you shouldn't.

See *Dialect, Sex.*

▼
PSYCHIC DISTANCE

○ Psychic distance is the degree of intimacy readers feel toward characters in the fiction. A story that starts

> A young man and a young woman sat morosely under a green parasol. They seemed mutually peeved.

has its readers looking at the characters from the outside, almost as if they were animals being observed in a human zoo. But if the story starts

> Philip stared unhappily across the table. The honeymoon was not going well at all.

readers are virtually inside the character.

Distance is created by such techniques as establishing a cool and dispassionate narrative voice and summarizing much of the action, dialogue, and thoughts of the characters. The effect is often to diminish the importance and uniqueness of individual lives. It is as if the readers are somewhat God-like, looking down from above on the mortals with their troubles and foibles.

When writers are self-conscious about themselves as writers they often keep a great distance from their characters, sounding as if they were writing encyclopedia entries instead of stories. Their hesitancy about physical and psychological intimacy can be a barrier to vital fiction.

Conversely, a narration that makes readers hear the characters' heavy breathing and smell their emotional anguish diminishes distance. Readers feel so close to the characters that, for those magical moments, they *become* those characters.

See *Immediacy, Narrator, Point of View.*

▼

READING

○   We read for delight, for insight, for thrills, and for comfort. But how do we read as writers?

The answer is—differently. Some writers read gingerly, fearful of being overwhelmed by the eloquence of others and losing confidence in their own powers. Others read savagely, looking for weaknesses that betray the inadequacies of the text and its creator. Many writers won't read while they're writing for fear of echoing the voice of the book they are reading. Others are afraid of finding that their own territory has already been worked over. But some writers love to read. They aren't intimidated or inhibited by writers, whether classic or contemporary. They are inspired as their own imaginations leap up at the achievements of others.

As a writer you can read in the traditional way, giving yourself over to the fictional world, getting caught up in the characters' lives, suffering with them, and sharing their emotions and adventures. Or you can read more analytically, trying to understand how these writers handle the problems of narration, how they make time pass, make characters memorable, or embed their own social observations. You can learn a great deal from this kind of reading. You begin to see the devices writers use to make scenes and dialogue vivid or to get into the minds of their characters, and you recognize that it is a magic you can learn yourself.

This history of art gives a useful model. As Western artists discovered how to handle perspective, anatomy, and light, they learned from one another. They built on their predecessors, refining, modifying, or even inverting established techniques.

Literary artists, especially writers of fiction, have a similar situation as they observe the fictional strategies other writers have evolved. Laurence Sterne manipulated time. Charles Dickens managed multiple plot lines. Gustave Flaubert manipulated point of view. James Joyce lyricized narrative. John Dos Passos created collages. Virginia Woolf used internal consciousness. Anaïs Nin exploited dreams. Jorge Borges turned philosophy into stories. Ralph Ellison uses a blues structure. Renata Adler fractures narrative. Milan Kundera juggles themes. Writers can show you the way and inspire you with further possibilities. You learn from the solutions of others.

Writers need not reinvent these literary wheels. They aren't rules, they're tools. Your reading can liberate your writing.

See *Novel, Plot.*

▼

REALISM

As a philosophical term, *realism* raises complex issues, such as What is real? Is everything? Is nothing? Am I? Are you? How can I know? and other late-night ponderings. But since the nineteenth century, realism accumulated specific meanings that are important for a writer to understand. Realism became associated with a type of fiction that argued that art was not only about extraordinary events, amazing places, and spectacular characters, but could be fashioned from everyday life. Realism justified fiction that stressed accurate observation of characters, scenes, events, and problems that are familiar to regular folks.

Realists felt they were doing more serious work than the writers of wild adventure stories and improbable love stories, whom they called Romanticists, because realists tried to show how people actually lived and suffered and dealt with their problems. The story of a kid growing up in Mississippi was as much a subject for great art as the story of a European prince; a salesman was as significant as a tycoon. Realism demonstrated that relatively simple plots could be effective structures for long works. As in seventeenth-century Dutch genre painting, beauty lay in the ordinary surroundings and rituals of human existence. Realism recognized a responsibility to record the more mundane and less admirable aspects of daily life. Most important, it let you perceive that your own region, your own background, and your own experience were fit subjects for art. That remains one of realism's strongest legacies.

American realists of the nineteenth century were limited in a number of ways. Since many knew only middle-class life, that was all that was real to them. They were prudish, and their treatment of sex tended to be anything but "real." Generally committed to an optimistic view of life, they sometimes could not deal with the tragic implications of their own subjects. You could say they violated their own premises by limiting the notion of what is real. But other realists came along who knew of poverty and prisons, violence and brutality.

Realism no longer means limiting yourself to the small trials and tribulations of middle-class life. For one thing, we know that middle-class life is not filled with small trials and tribulations but, as John Cheever recorded, with alcoholism and suicide, with break-ins and breakdowns. Our whole sense of what is real has been transformed. Don DeLillo's nightmare world of toxic spills is on the nightly news. Our sense of subject matter has changed. Denis Johnson's murderous criminals seem as close to us as the people we pass on the street. The worlds of the schizophrenic, the addict, the political zealot—the people who have been pushed to the margins of society—are as real as the world at the center. Our ordinary lives are improbable.

Yet realism remains an important aesthetic principle. The lives you depict are powerful because they seem true, immediate, and real. The events may be bizarre, but they are believable, as in the fiction of Mary McGarry Morris or Alice McDermott, with their weird abductions and suburban riots. The plots might be twisted, but they seem to grow naturally out of the possibilities and dangers of the real world.

If you provide enough convincing information, your readers will accept the reality of your characters no matter how upsetting or outrageous their actions are. If you don't provide the information that gives insight into background and motivation, the characters seem made up, implausible. If readers find them "unbelievable" the problem might lie not in what they do, but in what the writer didn't do. In Flannery O'Connor's "A Good Man Is Hard to Find" she has the Misfit himself convince us of his horrifying reality.

Even in surreal fictions, which leave traditional realism far behind, realist principles inhere. Gogol and Kafka have their own accuracy and almost obsessive attention to detail. *Magical realism,* the term used to describe such works, combines the ordinary with the inexplicable. In works by writers like Gabriel García Márquez and Jorge Borges, Western rationality clashes with magical native cultures. In other writers' fictions it's the intermingling of the natural with the supernatural, the living with the dead. Each world is as real as the other. Before the invention of the term, America had its own magic realist tradition—starting with Poe, Hawthorne, and Henry James, and continuing in writers like Malamud, Pynchon, and even William Faulkner.

See *Accuracy, Naturalism, Places and Place Names, Premise, Trust Your Material,* "Write What You Know."

▼

RED HERRING

○ A red herring is something in a story that draws attention to itself but then turns out to have nothing to do with the story. When writers make a particular point of describing a deformed turtle, a locked closet, or a lurking girl, readers expect they are necessary to understand the piece. If they seem forgotten by the time the story is over, they are red herrings.

Red herrings often occur when writers have changed their minds about a story, or are fossils of ideas once part of earlier versions. To avoid this, revise carefully. As a story evolves, images that are no longer relevant to the end need to be trapped and extracted from the beginning.

Other varieties of red herrings include character red herrings, who seem important and then vanish from the story; plot red herrings, which start and get forgotten; and cheap-trick red herrings, wherein the writer deliberately misleads the reader into worrying merely to set up a bit of suspense.

See "Don't Do This," *Plot, Revision.*

▼

RESOLUTION

○   Resolution, when it's right for the particular material, brings the work to a satisfactory close.

In certain forms, like television situation shows, tight resolutions are standard. Everyone learns a lesson, makes a promise, or gets his or her just deserts in one way or another. In realistic fiction that kind of tight ending seems manipulated. Since life does not work out that neatly, fiction that does so falsifies life. However, in comic fiction, part of the fun might derive from an ingenious resolution that brings about desired but unexpected results. In other forms like romances, mysteries, and espionage novels, fairly tight resolutions are traditional, though a few loose ends can be intriguing.

In short fiction explicit resolutions are comparatively rare. A convincing change of personality is difficult to execute in a short space. It's an achievement if you simply show characters beginning to comprehend something significant, and do this plausibly and movingly. Usually the outcomes are implied. One reason for this is that the moment of insight, the epiphany, is often the high point of the story. Final scenes in which characters dramatically manifest new insights or overt changes of heart can feel anticlimactic or simplistic. Too tight a resolution makes the story seem pat, mechanical, and cliché.

See *Endings, Epiphany, Irony, Poetic Justice.*

▼

REVISION

○   A story that appears full-blown, finished, and completely realized in its first draft is rarer than the ninety-yard pass, the hole-in-one, or the sixty-foot basket. Those feats are almost miraculous exceptions to a general rule. For writers the general rule is revision. A story grows with each draft, finding itself, developing its textures, and eliminating what is extraneous. Revision is integral to the creative process. It is the work's discovery of itself.

Your first draft may be uninhibited, exploratory, and experimental. You must look at it closely, ponder it, and ask yourself certain questions: What am I trying to do? What is the heart of the matter? Why are all these characters here? Why are all these scenes here? Why did I start the story where I did? Why did I devote all that space to that scene? Why did I devote so little space to this scene? Why did I handle point of view that way? Is my narrative voice the way I want it?

Often first drafts start out as one story and turn into another. The second idea might be the real story and the first was warm-up. Or the first got sidetracked, and the second idea might make a good story, but not the good story you're working on now. Or there might be a single anecdote you now see is the heart of it all, the real story you want to tell.

Some writers get hung up on first-draft ideas, as if to abandon any one is to betray some primal creative impulse. "If I wrote it, it must be important." Other writers are too quick to cut their freshest passages. "Oh, that part's too weird." But it's the thoughtful shaping of these impulses that creates art. Fear of making decisions or an oversolicitous, doting fondness for your prose paralyzes your work. And it's a lack of trust in their individual vision that makes writers take out the best parts.

Another sort of frustration occurs when writers actually change their minds about what their stories are from draft to draft. Each revision is not a step forward but sideways. Each is a first draft of another possible story. This variety of the discovery process is confusing because the story is getting no closer to being finished. To bring your story to fruition, you have to choose one possibility and develop that.

Figuring out your own weaknesses takes thought and experience. Some people feel miserable when they're asked to revise because they don't really know how to tell which parts are fine and which parts need work, and they don't have any specific sense of what to do. But there are principles that can be learned; I guess that's what this book is mostly about.

Since revising is the discovery of the heart of the story, it's a progressive process; each revision brings you closer to success. And the closer you come, the more complete the story feels. Revision continues until you reach the point at which you feel you have done all you can to make the story as complete as it can be. It might not be perfect. You might know more later, but now is not later. Now is the time to send it out, to see if it flies.

See *Advice, Workshops.*

▼

ROMAN À CLEF

○ This term refers to a novel based on the lives of real people, but the names or other superficial details have been changed. If readers know the real-life situation, they have the key, so to speak (*clef* is "key" in French; *roman* means "novel"). Then they can tell who is supposed to be whom.

A true roman à clef might be a fictionalized but fairly accurate account. Aldous Huxley's *Point Counter Point* includes characters who are closely based on D. H. Lawrence and John

Middleton Murry. In *On the Road,* Jack Kerouac's characters resemble himself, Neal Cassady, William Burroughs, Allen Ginsberg, and other friends. A variant of the form (which perhaps should be called a "false roman à clef") implies that it is based on the lives of real people, but is, in fact, wildly fictionalized. Harold Robbins's *The Carpetbaggers* adapts incidents to create a specious resemblance to the lives of Howard Hughes and Jane Russell.

Many novels have characters that come from real life, and some novels are extremely autobiographical, but a roman à clef usually means that the entire novel is dominated by its appropriation of an identifiable set of publicly recognizable figures. If you have lived among interesting and famous people, a roman à clef is a way to recreate them as fictional characters. That allows you freedoms of interpretation and invention not available to conventional biographers. It also might involve you in complex lawsuits about exploitation of a person's "commercial value," libel, and invasion of privacy. See *Novel, Realism.*

▼

ROMANCE
:
○   Despite the apparent dominance of the realist novel, you can still write a romance. The question, though, is: What is a romance today? Romance has a long history in which it has meant a number of things: something not written in Latin, chivalric tales in Old French, stories of extraordinary and unusual happenings, and, lately, formulaic stories about love. Romance gives you the freedom to delve into the exotic, the bizarre, the fantastic, and the improbable.

In 1957, the critic Richard Chase in a book called *The*

American Novel and Its Tradition made an interesting argument. He proposed that the romance is the basic American form of fiction. By romance, he meant works that are filled with "radical forms of alienation, contradiction, and disorder." He found plenty of examples in great American writers like Melville, Hawthorne, Twain, James, and Fitzgerald. Chase contrasted that with the tradition of the English novel, which shows "harmony, reconciliation, catharsis, and transfiguration." It's a shrewd and imaginative observation. Many major American writers in the last thirty years seem full of alienation, contradiction, and disorder. Flannery O'Connor, John Hawkes, John Barth, Thomas Pynchon, Ursula Le Guin, Ishmael Reed, and Kurt Vonnegut have wide apocalyptic streaks. On the other hand, some of the best writing in America today seeks reconciliation and catharsis. You can see that in Anne Tyler, Toni Morrison, and Walker Percy. The moral for writers is that America is complex and contradictory. There is no school but the school you want to enroll in.

The romance, whether primeval, medieval, futuristic, zoological, or magical, whether based on the quest for love, power, or sheer adventure, has to deal with the problems all fiction must face. Your characters (whether heroes or monsters) need to be emotionally engaging. You need to create a continual sense of development and change in situation. Your story must be true to its own premises (whether natural or supernatural). And your language should be fresh and vital (though commercial fantasy writing seems to have a high tolerance for purple prose and clichés).

See *Melodrama, Realism, Sentimentality.*

▼
SATIRE

o   Traditionally, satire is said to use humor to attack evils in order to reform its objects of criticism. But satire is often neither humorous in the conventional sense nor very likely to bring about any change of heart or mind in its targets.

A more realistic definition of satire states that it uses the oblique strategies of art to expose the foolishness or iniquity in various practices, ideas, and people. It ranges from mild and playful to corrosive and violent. Subjects range from the minor irritations of everyday life to the major brutalities of governments and gods. Strategies include exaggeration, irony, caricature, parable, fable, burlesque, sarcasm, and ingenuousness.

A satire's criticism needs to be in proportion to the object of the satire. That is, it doesn't work to express great moral outrage over the popularity of shoulder pads, the vulgarity of underarm deodorant commercials, or the misuse of the word *hopefully*. The object there is to make people aware, to get them to laugh at themselves, and perhaps be more conscious of the follies of their world.

But serious satirists like Jonathan Swift, who wrote about the cruelty of religious wars, or Mark Twain, who wrote about the monstrousness of the slave trade, tend not to be funny. They use devices like caricature and exaggeration, but the caricatures are magnified and the exaggerations intensified. They express an indignation so strong that language can barely contain it, and good manners or matters of tastefulness seem pitifully irrelevant. William Burroughs writes of a society he thinks is so obscene that only obscenity can express it.

If you write satire you must balance criticism and humor. If you're too upset, the work becomes a diatribe, not a satire. If you're too amused, you seem to be condoning what you want to condemn. Lately, satirists complain of being overtaken by history—they invent wild exaggerations, and find them happening in the next day's headlines.

Satirists tend to be most perceptive and successful when they deal with their own country, their own class, their own circle. A satiric novel needs to keep readers' attention as other novels do—through intriguing characters, lively plots, and interesting situations. The most pervasive device of the satiric novel is not laughter—it's a wry humor wreathed with barbed insights and structured on danger, escape, and death. That was true of Jonathan Swift's *Gulliver's Travels,* Mark Twain's *Huckleberry Finn,* and Franz Kafka's *The Trial,* and it's true of Kurt Vonnegut's *Player Piano,* Tom Wolfe's *Bonfire of the Vanities,* and Milan Kundera's *Book of Laughter and Forgetting.*

Satirists have a particularly interesting problem—being completely misunderstood. Would-be satirists write to their newspaper attacking sexism or atomic warfare with ironic praise. Then a swarm of letters attacks them for being sexists or nuclear nuts. Daniel Defoe went to jail because his satire was misunderstood. The successful satirist must embed enough information so that her point is not overwhelmed, and she must make sure she is not swallowed by her own satire.

See *Comedy, Parody.*

▼
SCENE

○ A child in a tantrum screams, throws toys, lies on the floor, and kicks the air. The parents say, "You're making a scene!" It's a tremendously suggestive phrase for writers. When you "make a scene" you create a memorable moment. You interrupt normal patterns. The scene gets remembered as a significant event in a life history. "When we took you to the zoo, you refused to leave the elephant house. You made such a scene."

As a writer you have the same opportunity—to stop time, create an event, make a scene. Your readers can be made to feel the drama of a moment. Actions and thoughts that take seconds to happen in life may take paragraphs, even pages, to be told. When Huck Finn decides he'll take his chances on eternal damnation rather than betray his friend Jim, Twain doesn't just tell it—he makes a scene.

When you want to make a scene in your own writing, render sensations fully so that readers cringe at the slap in the face, hear the whimper of pain, see her elbow hit the blue chair, and feel your character's rage and frustration. Use direct dialogue, physical reactions, gestures, smells, sounds, and thoughts.

Fully rendered scenes are emotional high points. If a novel never compresses action, never summarizes, but is all in full-blown scenes, the endless dialogue and details get monotonous. A shopping trip takes as long as a showdown. It's as if the writer doesn't know what is important and what's not. Remember the wisdom of the child: Make a scene when you really want everyone's full attention.

See *Description, Dialogue, Mise-en-scène, Showing and Telling.*

▼

SCIENCE FICTION

o   This is a form of genre writing that ranges from intellectual speculation on the nature of existence to the corniest intergalactic spaceship yarns. Some science fiction writers are interested in the effects of technology, the possible forms of new societies, the direction of contemporary culture, the frontiers of science, and ingenious concepts that expand the reader's mind. Other science fiction writers focus on superhuman characters, melodramatic escapades, and highly complicated plots.

The best writers of science fiction, such as Philip Dick, Ursula Le Guin, and Harlan Ellison, understand the principles of crafting an authoritative style, of creating interesting characters, and of telling an arresting story. In their search for fresh ideas, they keep up with scientific research, not only in astrophysics, but in neurobiology, genetics, psychology, and anthropology. Journals like *Science, Science News,* and *Brain / Mind* are a constant source of inspiration.

See *Genre.*

▼

SENTIMENTALITY

o   When writers try to manipulate their readers by making them feel emotions that the writers haven't honestly earned, we call the work sentimental. Certain situations will make readers teary-eyed—the death of a child, the reunion of long-lost loved ones, the call to action of a group of unjustly oppressed people, the cruel disappointment of an old person, the self-sacrifice of a courageous animal. Using such scenes is like pushing a button that causes an emotional reflex.

Readers value fiction that moves them emotionally but may resent being set up and manipulated. Some stories, like those involving loss and grief, love and death, are intrinsically deeply touching. In those cases, it's more effective to use restraint in your telling and to avoid overemphasizing what readers are already feeling.

Dwelling on the emotion alone seems self-indulgently sentimental. These stories just tell us how bad the character felt—how dark, how sad, how miserable, how pained, how gloomy. Some stories, especially those involving situations like the loss of a loved one, have been told so often that writers have a hard time making readers see them as anything but clichés. But a story can save itself from sentimentality by insight, humor, freshness, and specificity (perhaps even a dead pet story).

There have been interesting changes in attitudes toward the sentimental in fiction. Eighteenth- and nineteenth-century fiction emphasized sentimentality and often devoted itself to precipitating a good cry. This emphasis fades from serious literature in the twentieth century, when sentimentality is seen as cheap, melodramatic, and unsophisticated. The change may be due to the overexploitation of sentimental devices, not only in best-selling books, but in theater, movies, television, and popular song. Though sentimentality might not be admired, it's still dear to the heart of a vast audience (and pays its creators far better than irony likely ever will).

See *Bathos, Cliché,* "Don't Do This."

▼
SEX

○ Love and sexual relationships have long been central subjects for writers. But in serious fiction, graphic descriptions of sexual contact have been pretty much absent until fairly recently. Writers of the early twentieth century, like James Joyce, D. H. Lawrence, and Anaïs Nin, established that all human activity was an appropriate subject, and liberated fiction from prudery and false modesty.

The liberation from censorship produced a huge popular literature and generated a vast swarm of sexual clichés to describe beautiful women, beautiful men, sexual activities, and physical responses. Breasts stood erect, male organs throbbed, lips quivered, and nipples hardened like diamonds. Anyone writing today is aware of the difficulties of avoiding such clichés. Also you have your own reticence and modesties to contend with. When you write about sexual activity, you become acutely aware of your own ambivalence about making private intimacies public.

A particularly vexing problem is what words to use. Sexual activities have a vocabulary range from lyric to coarse and from polite to obscene, so there usually is appropriate language. Characters can want to make love, mess around, play house, or get laid. Sexual parts, however, have names that sound either clinical (penis), childish (wee-wee), vulgar (cock), or porno-euphemistic (tower of power). Often nothing sounds right. This is probably the best rule: If the description is in the narrative voice, use the term that the narrator would use. If it's a character thinking or talking, the character's vocabulary is what you should stay with. That gives a chance to

show the character's directness or squeamishness, sophisti-
cation or remoteness.

You might keep in mind that you're trying to create your
character's feelings and experience. This is no time to be an
intrusive narrator providing clinical description. Tell what your
character is thinking, is worrying about, is feeling. The most
effective details are those most unexpected. If she notices a
small line of clogged follicles along his thigh, that's part of
her experience. If he's remembering a girl he kissed in the
seventh grade, that's part of his. If he feels a delirium of pleasure, render those sensations. Is your character distracted,
uneasy, guilty, or transported? What thoughts are really
occurring? Paradoxically the most telling aspect of sexual
activity is what goes on in the characters' heads.

See *Character, Negative Positive Knowledge, Profanity/
Obscenity.*

▼

SHORT NOVEL

○ The short novel is the form of some of our
finest fiction. Its length varies greatly, from what some would
call long short stories to what others would think of as novels. Kafka's "Metamorphosis" and Voltaire's *Candide* both
appear in anthologies of short novels. From 15,000 to 50,000
words seem to be outside limits.

Writers like D. H. Lawrence, Joseph Conrad, Henry James,
and Katherine Anne Porter found that the short novel gave
them space to develop satisfying complexity within a scale
that lent itself to an artful shaping of the work. You can deal
with a bigger piece of time, more characters, and more scenes,

as in Henry James's *Daisy Miller* or Toni Morrison's *Sula*. Yet at the same time, the short novel doesn't get baggy and long-winded as fat novels often do. There's no place readers can skip and skim.

But the short novel remains a problematical form, difficult to classify, and, worst of all from your point of view, extremely difficult to market. Magazines don't want them because they're too long. Book publishers don't want them because they're too short. Lately, as Saul Bellow and Jane Smiley have shown, shorter novels have been gaining in popularity, sometimes as leadoffs for short-story collections and sometimes as separate publications (Philip Roth provides examples of both).

See *Novel, Short Story, Structure.*

▼

SHORT STORY

○   Attempts to define the short story seem to be of more interest to critics than to writers. In books on the short story, you can find distinctions between tales, fables, yarns, sketches, anecdotes, and something the critic will posit as the true short story. Ultimately, definitions might as well read, "A short story is what feels like a short story." If you read definitions of short stories that have been written over the decades, it is easy to see that what was indispensable for one generation is considered archaic in the next.

So what advice can be offered to writers today? First, how long should a short story be? Writers have pushed at these limits by writing short stories that are fewer than 100 words long and more than 15,000 words long. Most short stories published today seem to run between 2,000 and 7,000 words. The longer the story, the more space it takes, and the more the editors have to love it to make that commitment. The shorter the story, the easier it is for an editor to assent to it. That doesn't mean you should write stories that are shorter than you want. It just means that some muses present more problems than others.

Second, start fast. These are impatient times. Readers will give you about two paragraphs. If nothing happens by that time, they're gone.

Third, make sure what you have is a story. But what is a story? If you read widely, you'll find stories that read like essays, like sketches, like anecdotes, like reminiscences, like poetic descriptions, like condensed novels, like movie scenarios, madman's monologues, cubist collages, like lots of things. So what is a story? The most pragmatic definition is: A story is what the editor says is a story. A tradition-minded editor might have some very specific criteria in mind, such as "I want to see conflict, resolution, and a change in the main character." A nontraditional editor might say, "Anything is a story as long as it's interesting."

I would say this: *A story is what happens to the reader.*

Whatever methods or anti-methods, structures or un-structures you choose, it is a story if something happens to your readers. By *something* I mean something that's emotionally and intellectually moving enough to have some gravity, some weight, some sense of significance. By *happens* I mean makes an impression, causes a reaction, precipitates a thought, creates a mood. A *story* makes readers feel that they have had an experience, whether the story's form is traditional or strange, whether the narrator explains its meaning or lets it lie on the plate.

If you feel free to explore possibilities, you are likely to discover ways of making things happen for your readers that have not been part of previous formulations or definitions. The test for a story lies in its effect, not its method.

See *Beginnings, Endings, Plot, Short Novel, Tension.*

▼

SHOWING AND TELLING

○ The distinction between showing and telling has become part of the vocabulary of every writing teacher in America. It tends to be stated this way:

> Showing is good and telling is bad. You are not *showing* me the way the character feels. You are just *telling* me how the character feels.

This means that the writer has not rendered the sensations or thoughts in enough detail. In *telling*, a character is merely described:

> Willis was mean and stupid, but he was shrewd too.

In *showing*, the character *is* what you say he is:

> Willis put his fist in my face. "I'm dumb, huh? I'm an idiot, huh? So I punch you in the mouth and then I'm not so dumb. Right?"
> I had to admit his argument had a curious logic.

If you simply *tell* that your character has broken a leg, the reader doesn't feel it. If you *show* the bare bone sticking through pale skin, the reader experiences it. The distinction becomes very important when dealing with mental states. If you say your character is depressed, but she doesn't think depressed, doesn't talk depressed, doesn't act depressed, your readers won't feel or believe she's depressed.

The principle *show don't tell* has much truth to it. But it becomes a trap for writers who don't recognize that every great writer does considerable telling along with showing. Showing—that is, rendering sensation in detail—takes a lot of space. It means making a scene so that readers feel each moment of fictional time as if it were really happening. Good writing doesn't want to do that all the time.

Telling can be efficient, crisp, and, given some attention to phrasing, evocative. It's a way of summarizing, of commenting, and of embedding insights and reflections. You could have a scene in which you show Thayer cheating a rich, potentially lucrative customer, and through the dialogue make the reader gradually see that Thayer doesn't think about how much more he could make if he were honest. But if Thayer is a minor character you might not want to write a whole scene for him. You might simply want to introduce him by telling readers:

> Thayer was an oily, corrupt little guy who would rather make fifty dollars by lying to you than a hundred by telling the truth.

The notion that showing is good and telling is bad is a misleading oversimplification. Each has its place. Read John Cheever's stories. Scene and summary—showing and telling—create a rhythm for the dance of fiction.

See *Dialogue, Scene.*

▼

STEREOTYPE

○ This negative term is used when writers create characters whose traits have so little individuality that readers are merely reminded of how often they've seen that type done before. A stereotype is a particular form of cliché.

Writers often respond to the charge by conjuring up reality. Perhaps a story has a high school principal who is a pompous, rigid, overweight person in a bow tie who fails to understand his students and thinks them worthless.

"A stereotype," say the readers.

"But I know a person just like this," argues the writer. The writer may be telling the truth, but if readers feel a character is a stereotype, it means that the writer has not perceived anything *new*, that she has simply described the obvious traits. The writer is unaware of her own cultural bias—she's finding only what she's been taught to see. Therefore, the character, even though based on life, doesn't come alive as an individual.

If a major character is a stereotype, the entire work is in serious trouble. Minor characters give you more leeway. A talkative taxicab driver or an inattentive salesperson might seem familiar and true rather than stereotypical. Still, you should ask yourself, even when creating a little scene with a bartender or banker or hitchhiker: What am I bringing to this? What am I observing that will strike my readers as fresh? Am I only fulfilling readers' preconceptions? Stereotyped characters based on racial, ethnic, gender, or social-class prejudice are not only clichéd, they're offensive.

See *Archetype, Character, Cliché, Sentimentality.*

▼
STORIES WITHIN STORIES

○   Good fiction is full of good fiction. Interesting short stories often contain many embedded stories. The narrator tells little stories about the characters. Characters remember through stories. Characters talk to each other by telling stories. These embeddings are rich with possibility. The stories can characterize the teller, advance the plot, and introduce ideas. But most important, they enliven the texture of the entire narrative.

Stories within stories can be as short as a single sentence:

> When I was about nine these two bigger kids stopped me and asked me did I have a wiggler, and when I said I didn't know, they just laughed.

They can be several sentences:

> Alice remembered how her dad would order in Omega, the luncheonette they ate in every Saturday. "Hot dog on a bun, hold the bun. Iced tea, hold the ice," and they'd both smile happily.

Longer stories within stories are risky. Writers like John Barth and John Irving take particular delight in overtly embedding stories within their novels. But these stories have to be gripping enough so that readers don't say, "Get on with the *real* story." Placement, pace, and length need careful planning. Readers have to be convinced that the story you are telling at that moment *is* the real story.

See *Character, Facade, Flashback, Interior Monologue, Juggling, Point of View.*

▼

STREAM OF CONSCIOUSNESS

○ Stream of consciousness is the deepest immersion into the mind of a character. Stream-of-consciousness writing simulates the images, memories, sensations, and thoughts that flow through the brain before the rational mind sorts them out, represses what it can't deal with, discards what it thinks irrelevant, and turns everything into what's called logical thinking. The art in writing stream-of-consciousness prose lies in presenting that unmediated flow, that seeming chaos, so that it still makes sense to readers. Among the thought fragments, childhood images, bits of dreams, and present sensations, you need to insert enough information so that readers feel not baffled, but magically inside another person's mind and body.

To create this jumble of simultaneous brain activity, break up conventional syntax—use sentence fragments, single images, and individual words. Intermingle thoughts and impulses—immediate and distant, subconscious and conscious, past and present.

Bullying is what she might like. Pick on her. Pick on. The schoolyard. You're a little fat. Here and here. Dimple knees. Get off me. Let me go. You're all so stupid. I'll show you. I'll show her. Don't tell me you don't know what zabaglione is. I don't believe it. What about panzanelle? I thought you'd been to Italy. Pasta, pasta. Pasta, basta. This whole thing isn't worth it.

Stream-of-consciousness writing gives readers the most intimate possible knowledge of the character, the deepest, most vulnerable, most private self. Stream of consciousness presents problems too, for it lends itself to retrospection and dramatic stasis. The mind swims backward and readers want to go forward.

The most interesting example of a work drowning in the deep stream of consciousness is Marguerite Young's great, ambitious, unread novel, *Miss MacIntosh, My Darling*. Probably the most memorable, successful use of stream of consciousness is the famous Molly Bloom section of James Joyce's *Ulysses*.

See *Documents / Diaries / Letters, Interior Monologue*.

▼

STRUCTURE

o Structure refers to the overall design of the work. That often means plot. But it can mean thematic plan—for example, having chapters from alternating points of view, or going back and forth between present and past time. Or it can mean the number and length of chapters or books ("books" in the sense of subdivisions within a novel). For some writers, it means the way that turns in the action create a framework for the narrative.

In fiction, scale and structure are intimately related. The shorter the story, the more structural freedom you have. Over a few pages your readers' attention can be sustained by a meditation, a monologue, a piece of resonant description. A short story does have a structure. It's like a ball thrown in the air, or in a more complicated story, like several balls thrown in the air. The arc of the story creates a shape that carries your readers through the experience of the story.

But when your narrative has accumulated two hundred or five hundred pages, an enormous amount of energy must go into structural considerations, with calculations and manipulations about plots, subplots, and entrances and exits. Novelists who are not interested in thinking about these problems may have to wait for their reward in the next world. In this one, agents and editors may tell them that they write well, are sensitive and perceptive, but somehow what is there is not a novel. Oh, it has wonderful sections and passages, *but*—there's always a but. The manuscript lacks direction, they say, momentum, shape. It lacks structure.

Short-story writers are jewelers, sharpshooters, photographers, and jugglers. Novelists must be symphony composers, stage magicians, but above all, engineers and architects. Short-story writers can illuminate in a flash; they can hit-and-run. Novelists must create successions of mysteries and solutions, deploy chains of intrigants and cliff-hangers, develop momentum, sustain suspense, provide variation, and bring it all to a satisfying conclusion.

See *Beginnings, Endings, Freytag's Pyramid, Novel, Plot, Position, Resolution, Short Story, Suspense.*

▼

STYLE

○ Style is how you tell your story. People often talk about the style and subject of a work of art as if they were separable. But if you think about it, the real subject of Van Gogh's landscapes is how he painted the landscapes and the subject of Cézanne's still lifes is how he painted the peaches.

So, too, in literature—the subject of Hemingway's stories is not fishing, but how he wrote about fishing, and the subject of Faulkner's novels is not the South, but how he wrote about the South. *How,* in the case of writers, means what perceptions, what emotions, what insights, what frames of reference, what worlds they see and create through their words. So advice on style would be literally advice on everything that has to do with writing.

However, when we talk about "writing style" we generally mean decisions about brush strokes rather than subject matter and structure. Style in this sense has more to do with individual words, sentences, and paragraphs than with entire chapters and books.

So let's start with some specifics. The smallest unit of style is the words you choose. The possibilities range from sticking as close as possible to everyday speech:

> Frajool was a mean, nasty low-life. If he couldn't beat you he'd cheat you.

to a deliberately esoteric vocabulary:

> Frajool was an incorrigibly maleficent cur; if he couldn't conquer he'd cozen.

You can deploy specialized vocabularies. If you have your characters climbing about monadnocks or dissecting liverworts or securing halyards, the words both establish the subject and lend authority to the writing. Some writers will avoid words like *azure* or *cerulean,* which seem old-fashioned. Others will avoid phrases like *maximize potential* or *intertextual overdetermination,* which seem soul-destroying. Your word choice is similar to a color choice for a painter. You take your words from a particular frame of reference—the street, the farm, the corporation, the academy. Some writers deliberately limit themselves to the diction of an ordinary person, others give themselves a richer vocabulary, and still others scour the *Oxford English Dictionary* for words like *farfalla* or *horrisonant* to dazzle or delight their readers.

What should you do? You should be comfortable with your vocabulary. If you feel constrained by your lack of knowledge of vocabulary, or you can't remember the word you want, use your dictionaries, thesauruses, and synonym finders. These books act as extensions of your mind. At the same time, don't underestimate yourself. Your strongest, most direct language is probably already part of you. Trusting the words you know is often better than importing a vocabulary not your own.

Phrases and sentences also create style. Some sentences are boring and awkward. They are not taut. They meander:

> They look as if they are about to end but then go on to add another prepositional phrase to a sentence that seems done by this time but it turns out that it isn't and the writer has another point he would like to make and still say one more thing before finally letting go.

When editors say they have to read only one or two pages of a 600-page novel to know they don't want to read any more, that seems cruel and irresponsible to the beginning writer. But editors can see from a small sample whether or not a writer has control of his words and sentences. Adverbs litter the constructions, words repeat themselves as if they forgot their earlier appearance, coordinating conjunctions proliferate, phrases wander about looking for something to dangle off. These things tell editors not to go on.

Opening sentences not only need to be grammatically correct and graceful, they also need to attract readers by their syntactical authority. Some writers start by using a direct expository sentence that commands attention and establishes a world. E. L. Doctorow begins *Ragtime:*

> In 1902 Father built a house at the crest of the Broadview Avenue Hill in New Rochelle, New York.

It's as straightforward and economical as Philip Roth's opening for *Goodbye, Columbus:*

> The first time I saw Brenda she asked me to hold her glasses.

Others start by using a phrase that is deliberately a bit askew in order to suggest that the fictional world will be unusual. Mark Helprin begins the opening story of his *Ellis Island* collection:

> In Munich are many men who look like weasels.

The deliberate awkwardness signals strangeness.

In *Play It As It Lays* Joan Didion's abruptness is instantly unsettling:

> What makes Iago evil? some people ask. I never ask.

Some writers attract attention by long, ingeniously fabricated sentences that wind their way around far longer than expected, dropping in all sorts of peripheral information, and when they seem as if they have completely lost track of themselves, they wrap themselves up and leave readers right in the palm of the smiling writer. Faulkner's *Sartoris* begins:

> As usual, old man Falls had brought John Sartoris into the room with him, had walked the three miles in from the county Poor Farm, fetching, like an odor, like the clean dusty smell of his faded overalls, the spirit of the dead man into that room where the dead man's son sat and where the two of them, pauper and banker, would sit for a half an hour in the company of him who had passed beyond death and then returned.

Other writers establish authority by opening with deliberately mysterious dialogue or a string of intriguing phrases. As Nabokov does:

> Lolita, light of my life, fire of my loins. My sin, my soul. Lo-lee-ta: the tip of the tongue taking a trip of three steps down the palate to tap, at three, on the teeth. Lo. Lee. Ta.

You are making a world out of sentences. Those sentences can be long or short, colloquial or literary, dense with description and imagery or spare and direct. Hemingway does not *just* write short sentences. And Faulkner does not *just* write long sentences. It's how often they write each, as well as the range of vocabulary they choose, that creates their different styles. Your sentences create the rhythm of your fictional world.

Paragraphs should be mentioned here because writers often fail to realize that the visual appearance of their pages is part of their writing. Very short paragraphs create a lively appearing fast-moving page. Very long paragraphs with large blocks of description and retrospection suggest a ruminative style. Varying the lengths of paragraphs creates a visual rhythm that can correspond to what is happening in the story.

You need to be comfortable with your style. Beginning writers often reach for a style they think is dignified and literary. They use ponderous words, complicated constructions, and images that sound as if they wanted to be in leather-bound books. This is not the writer's voice but a kind of literary collage of secondhand voices out of childhood reading, popular novels, old poems, and a notion that literature is something intoned by people in purple velvet robes lolling around a gigantic fireplace in an old mansion. There are writers, too, who want to appear witty and arch, or earthy and tough, when that's not who they are.

Finding your own style is a process of recognizing what is secondhand, what is someone else's style, and listening at the same time for your natural style. Though one thinks of style as something that is inevitably written, it is also oral, the spoken language with all its spontaneity and naturalness and surprise. Spoken language is what you listen for with your inner ear. The rhythms of the sentences, the lively syntax, the choice of words—all speak directly and persuasively to the reader. Look at the way Anton Chekhov or Willa Cather or Isaac Bashevis Singer or Flannery O'Connor begins a story. "They are so literary," you say. That's right, but listen to their openings and you will hear them as spoken voices.

Finding your own style means not falling under the spell of

another style. This is a real problem. Writers like Joyce, Faulkner, Woolf, Salinger, and Pynchon, writers with powerful distinctive styles, are seductive to their admirers. Ann Beattie's casual minimalism, Tom Robbins's free-floating commentary-fiction, or Jay McInerney's street-flash have similar attractions. Writers think, This is great, I love this, I want to write this way. But the result is that instead of being admired, the fiction is seen as derivative, secondhand. You might have to treat some of your favorite authors as you do those lovable but overbearing friends who will take over your life if you let them.

You can learn from these writers, however. See how their styles work. What rhythms of language are involved? How do long sentences keep their poise? What tension keeps a lyric voice from collapsing? How are complicated digressions kept lively? The more deeply you understand the style, the more you can learn—not to imitate it, but to see how to find your own style.

Comparison will be inevitable if influence is genuine, but it need not be invidious comparison. Writers can be acknowledged as in a tradition. Eudora Welty and numerous other writers point to the King James version of the Bible as the most important influence on their style. Raymond Carver acknowledged his debt to Ernest Hemingway.

Style is revealing, as handwriting is said to be. Henry James reveals his ruminative character in sentences that endlessly qualify themselves, modifying each preceding thought which is not *quite* right. Sherwood Anderson's belief in expressing the secrets of the human heart results in sentences that have the simplicity and directness of a child's voice.

Style can also reveal problems writers don't know they have.

If a writer isn't sure what to say about a character or scene, the reader can often feel the vagueness or reticence in the text. Dialogue might get squeamish or coy or artificially breezy. Discomfort with a subject is sometimes shown by stilted word choices, by the use of terms like "enamored of" instead of "love," by elaborate passive constructions and roundabout language:

> The sounds and smells of car traffic with the honking horns and exhaust fumes from the trucks and buses were always an irritant to Beth, who, after an arduous day's work, was filled with fatigue.

Instead of directness:

> Cars honked at trucks. Trucks honked back. Bus fumes stung her eyes. Beth felt miserable. It had been another long damn day and now this.

Style reveals prejudices. For example, readers might notice that whenever the writer describes a woman, it's in terms of her figure. Or minority characters might always be described in terms of their ethnic or racial characteristics instead of as individuals. Don't be defensive if something like that is pointed out in your own writing. Look to see if your language does reveal some unconscious prejudices. As far as the printed page is concerned, your style is who you are. (You are what you write?)

The more noticeable the style, the more the writer says, "Look at me!" The narrator, instead of staying out of view, edges out on stage and becomes a character. These writer / narrators sometimes take over in order to assault the conventions of fiction, reveal the inadequacy of language, expose the collapse of empirical reality, analyze the paradoxes in what they just said, comment upon their commentary, and prove that the writer doesn't exist and probably neither does the reader.

See *Cliché, Diction, Imagery, Motif, Narrator, Point of View, Revision, Texture, Voice.*

▼

SUBTLETY

○ Serious writers, including serious comic writers, are interested in subtlety, in avoiding heavy-handed effects and obvious characterizations. They want to make readers pay close attention, and readers enjoy picking up on clues as subtle as a hesitation or a dropped glance.

But popular fiction is often based on extremely unsubtle effects. Heroes and villains are drawn in sharp extremes. Relationships between characters are reiterated. Characters are created by repeating a certain cluster of adjectives. Thus we are told that a character is tempestuous and passionate, passionate and tempestuous, wild and passionate, wild and tempestuous, and that character rarely appears in the book without a reference to these traits. The reader, through sheer repetition, accepts the character as tempestuous. In fact, in best-selling popular fiction, repetition is no flaw. The reader is continually reminded who the heroine (or hero) is secretly in love with and what reservations the beloved has about fulfilling the lover's tempestuous desire.

The premium on subtlety can be a trap for writers, who—in order to avoid being obvious or repetitive—become fearful and anemic, as if they were more concerned with their image as fine and subtle people than in telling a story. Instead of finding appropriate ways to imply as much as possible, such writers wind up hardly having implied anything. These writers worry too much about telling rather than showing, and don't let their characters reveal enough.

That notion of subtlety is a mistake. Subtlety means being as richly informative as possible within the fabric of the narrative. Writers like John Cheever and Anne Tyler bury important thematic statements in the middle of paragraphs, give important insights to minor characters, and embed wisdom in jokes or seemingly pointless anecdotes. Subtlety lies in the adroitness with which you embed perceptions in the text.

See *Character, Endings, Irony, Narrative.*

▼

SUSPENSE

○ Suspense is the way you make your audience worry. Suspense gets readers to keep turning pages.

Suspense is the intense anxiety created by raging forest fires, stalking killers, and races to the bank to deposit the money minutes before the bank forecloses on the mortgage. But all narratives need to create suspense in some way, whether your material involves a ticking time bomb or a troubled marriage.

Comic writing depends on suspense. Will the feuding couple recognize that they belong together before either one does something really stupid? Will the good, bumbling lad be unjustly expelled from the school?

Serious writing depends on suspense. The stakes may be life or death, love or loss, insight or blindness. Whether you look at Jane Austen or Dostoyevsky, Thomas Hardy or Alice Walker, you'll find suspense. As a reader you nervously want to know what happens next, hoping for one resolution and fearing others.

Tension underlies suspense. Plot, pacing, intrigants, cliff-hangers, zigzags, partial disclosures of information, delicate situations, intimations of fear and hope—all are part of the orchestration of suspense.

But at the center of real suspense is character. Readers have to be emotionally involved before they can suffer your character's disappointments, be afraid when pain threatens, and hope fervently that when sweet Antonia's taxi is stuck in traffic, and it's raining, the policeman will let her through the train gate, to be reunited with her beloved Bernard before he returns to the darkness of Trondheim.

See *Character, Cliff-hanger, Intrigant, Plot, Position, Tension, Zigzag.*

▼

SUSPENSION OF DISBELIEF

○ This is the leap of faith readers make when they accept the special kind of truth and validity of a fictional world.

Usually a "willing suspension of disbelief" refers to unusual or unnatural circumstances: for example, a story set in the future or in a land where animals talk French. But readers also suspend disbelief in relation to the form of the fiction. They accept that Ken Kesey's silent Indian can tell *One Flew Over the Cuckoo's Nest* (complete with correct punctuation and chapter breaks), or that E. L. Doctorow can go into the minds of Emma Goldman or Harry Houdini in *Ragtime.*

The premises you establish in the beginning hint to the readers what to expect. If you make clear that the story is about a world ruled by the conventional laws of probability, it's difficult to get readers to suspend their disbelief in the last chapter and accept a highly improbable ending. William Dean Howells ruined several of his novels at their conclusions by contriving accidents to kill off inconvenient characters. If a narrative is set in a land of magic, writers have more latitude, but even magic has its rules. Tim O'Brien's hallucinatory intermingling of fact and fantasy in *Going After Cacciato* is created in the first chapter. The novel's scenes, whether in caverns under Vietnam or on the streets of Paris, are consistent with its premises.

If the work remains true to itself, readers will follow. But if you ask your readers to suspend their disbelief without regard to the premises of the story, they will stop suspending and start disbelieving.

See *Beginnings, Plot, Premise.*

▼

SYMBOLISM

o   Fiction writers can't help using symbolism; humans are always relating to each other symbolically. Such actions as shaking hands, kissing, and raising eyebrows symbolize relationships and attitudes. Clothing choices, like sandals with socks, or all-natural fibers, can symbolize a character's attitude toward society or a desired image. Foods, whether goat cheese rolled in mountain ash or proletarian black beans and rice, can manifest social aspirations. The progress of relationships can be symbolized by the giving of a book, a box of chocolates, a nightgown. A character's internal state may be expressed by the pictures on his walls.

Our culture has bestowed upon us a vast number of traditional symbols. Crucifixes, skulls, roses, and lambs. Fire, water, earth, and air. You can use these symbols conventionally, as in movies where all the villains wear black and the good guys, white. You can redefine the symbols, even reverse them, so that in a particular work the hero wears black or the pitchfork is associated with good, not evil. Rain, often a symbol of life, in Hemingway's *A Farewell to Arms* becomes associated with death.

Traditional symbols can seem like clichés. If you dress your self-sacrificing heroines in white muslin and the unscrupulous, scheming women in red satin, readers may assume that the other elements of the narrative will be similarly unoriginal. Reverse symbols can be another kind of cliché, the clichéd anti-cliché—the gruff pockmarked heroes and the baby-faced villains. Invented symbols can be so obscure that no one understands them. Writers who get caught up with "clever" symbols can be profoundly annoyed when no one notices them.

"Don't you see?" they say, " 'Maria went across the room.' Don't you get it? 'Across.' '*A cross!*' 'Maria.' '*Mary!*' It's a prefiguration."

"Oh," you say. "Yeah."

You can successfully create your own symbols within the work. Images, objects, and actions gather meaning through their use in the narrative. Flannery O'Connor's pea-green ties and artificial legs and cast-iron statues become symbolic through her carefully phrased descriptions, how they are seen by the characters, and their function in the plot.

Symbolism is neither a variety of artificial decoration nor a secret code. It's the word made flesh. It's the idea made visible. Writers are, after all, symbol-making animals.

See *Archetype, Cliché, Imagery, Metaphor and Simile, Objective Correlative, Stereotype.*

▼

TENSION

○ Tension is the mother of fiction. When tension and immediacy combine, the story begins.

Tension is created by conflict. The conflict might be between characters—how a young man seeks his freedom from his claustrophobic family, how a woman fights enemies to save her home. The conflict might be between your character and the forces of nature—how someone survives being lost in grizzly-bear country, or keeps from drowning when her boat capsizes. These conflicts are subject to endless variations: your character against forces earthly (Immigration Service bureaucrats) or unearthly (space viruses), technological machines (planes whose landing wheels have fallen off) or political machines (Germany or Tammany), the forces of repression (rigid priests and sadistic teachers) or the forces of anarchy (street gangs or lynch mobs), not to mention bad landlords, corrupt cops, loud neighbors, insurance salesmen, and vicious ex-lovers.

In much serious fiction, although the tension is high, the conflicts are psychological and philosophical. They might involve the character's quarrel with her religious faith, her ambivalence about her profession, her struggle to express her affection to those she loves. The traditional formulation that all fiction has three central conflicts (humans fight one another, nature, or themselves) is an interesting insight, but it's not that simple or separable. Characters don't merely face their enemies, they face themselves facing their enemies.

Writers are often unhappy with the idea that there must always be tension in a story, that a story is always about something that is wrong. "Why can't stories be happy?" they say. "Why can't a story be about a pleasant day at the beach with the family?" "Why do stories always have to be about troubled people and conflict?"

Perhaps one answer is that if you tell a story, you're implicitly saying to readers, "Listen to me, this is interesting. This is something different. This about something happening."

Readers take "something happening" to mean something out of the ordinary. Tension. Conflict. Confrontation.

"A story about a beautiful day at Palisades Amusement Park is out of the ordinary," the writer says. "It was a rare day, a wonderful day, a day when everything went right. Why isn't that a story?"

The writer's argument only makes our point stronger. His example *can* be a story. There is real tension in his re-creating that perfect day. When Wallace Stevens wrote, "Death is the mother of beauty," I think he meant that we value beauty because we know it is fleeting—the ripe fruit will soon rot, the beautiful person will inevitably die. If with every sentence of the Palisades Park story we feel the fragility of that day's beauty, the recognition of how exceptional it is, the way the characters transcend their everyday troubles, we feel the tension, and it will be a story.

Tension is inseparable from other aspects of storytelling. The more you involve readers with your character, the more tension they feel, so character development is crucial. The more intriguing the situation itself, the more interesting the tension, so plot development is crucial. The more you get readers to feel and visualize the scene, the more vivid the tension, so evocative detail is crucial. The more you make readers understand the significance of the outcome, the more tension is created, so thematic development is crucial.

At the end tension may be solved, dissolved, or resolved. Or it may not be. Some stories spoil themselves by trying to bring closure to that which can only stay open. The tension that lingers can make a story memorable.

See *Bear at the Door, Beginnings, Endings, Plot, Suspense, Zigzag.*

▼

TEXTURE
:
○   Texture is an aspect of style. It's created by such qualities as vocabulary choice, density of detail, complexity of imagery, and entry into the characters' minds.

Some writing is so densely textured that readers experience enormous amounts of information simultaneously on a number of different levels. Ishmael Reed starts *Mumbo-Jumbo:*

> A True Sport, the Mayor of New Orleans, spiffy in his patent-leather brown and white shoes, his plaid suit, the Rudolph Valentino parted-down-the-middle hair style, sits in his office. Sprawled upon his knees is Zuzu, local doo-wack-a-doo and the voo-do-dee-odo figzig. A slatternly floozy, her green, sequined dress quivers.

Other writing is stripped bare, as if to tell only one thing very simply. Barry Hannah begins *Ray:*

> Ray is thirty-three and he was born of decent religious parents, I say.

The possibilities are analogous to different styles of cooking—on the one hand we have complex dishes in which many sensations play against each other and, on the other, dishes that are so simple and natural that one pure flavor creates an experience.

One texture is not better than the other—the house of fiction has room for Thomas Pynchon's baroque layering and Raymond Carver's bareness. But you have to take care. Over-textured prose tries to do too much, crowds in so many sensations that all is blurred and effects are lost. Under-textured prose is just bland—the writer has omitted so much that there is no savor, nothing fresh or pungent to it. If texture vacillates, it feels as if the author can't decide what he's cooking.

What's important to remember is that the dish should be admired, not the cook. You don't want someone to say, "You are very clever," instead of, "This is delicious."

See *Diction, Motif, Style*.

▼

THEME

o   When literary critics use this term, they generally mean the idea or point of a work. Writers are often made uncomfortable by questions like, "What is the theme of your novel?" It seems reductive, like someone asking, "What is the bottom line on this thing?" Writers hope that people will read and think about their work, understanding it through that experience. Some writers respond evasively to questions about theme, saying things like, "It's just a story," or, as Mark Twain wrote in his notice preceding *The Adventures of Huckleberry Finn*, "Persons attempting to find a motive in this narrative will be prosecuted; persons attempting to find a moral in it will be banished; persons attempting to find a plot in it will be shot."

Other writers are more intellectual in their inspiration and more analytical about their creation. They clearly have a theme in mind, and their work is an exploration of a particular idea. Albert Camus or Jean-Paul Sartre used their fiction to discuss philosophical issues. Margaret Atwood and Robert Coover are explicitly interested in political themes.

If you want to explore philosophical, psychological, or social ideas in your fiction, think of theme as akin to character, setting, or imagery. Themes, like characters, can advance the plot, contribute to the tension, be attacked, and suffer ironic fates. John Barth made his themes the central characters in *End of the Road* and *Giles Goat-Boy*. Aesthetic ideas almost talk to each other in Julian Barnes's *Flaubert's Parrot*. Saul Bellow's characters embody themes.

Though many writers like to think of themselves primarily as storytellers, yarn spinners, and fabulists, themes and ideas are inevitable. Every work raises questions, examines possibilities, and imagines the consequences of actions. You can't avoid meaning even if you want to.

See *Character, Didacticism, Motif.*

▼

TITLE

o   Choosing a title is traumatic for some writers. They worry endlessly over being too heavy-handed, too obscure, too dull, too cute, and so forth. Nothing seems right. Part of the problem lies in the ambiguous status of the title.

It is both part of the artistry of the work and part of the advertising for the work. On the one hand, a good novel might need no title, and on the other, no one will want to read it if it doesn't have a title that sounds interesting.

Some solutions that have helped people are these. Take a title from a phrase in a scene that seems relatively unimportant. You have two friends in a car on the way to strong-arm someone into paying back a debt. Neither of your two characters is comfortable doing this. Chatting nervously as they drive by a pond, one guy says, "You see those ducks?" You think, That's my title, "Ducks." It plays around in the reader's mind; it's suggestive rather than definitive.

Or choose a title that simply states the place, the time, the name of an object or a character's profession. "Debt." That has an understated effect. It's intriguing, but it doesn't give anything away. Wonderful stories often have relatively plain, almost invisible titles. Writers who like to play with words often choose titles that have double meanings, one of which isn't apparent until the story has been read. A quotation from a literary work can be the source of a title that is appropriate, eloquent, and allusive. "Itself and Friends." The problem there is that, like epigraphs, the quotation may seem too familiar, too obscure, too pretentious, or too good (so your own work suffers in comparison).

Lists of possibilities created by free association and uncensored wildness help. Meditating over them leads to the breakthrough. Every child is finally named.

See *Names, Places and Place Names, Theme.*

▼

TOUR DE FORCE

○ A show of skill. Paganini wrote such difficult pieces for the violin that only he could play them. Dali painted details so minute that only magnifying glasses can reveal them.

Some writers are like literary pyrotechnicians, shooting off skyrockets of unusual imagery and magical effects. They tell stories in deliberately difficult ways and set themselves problems that require ingenious solutions. Nabokov, Pynchon, Kundera, and Borges are all on the high wire. Instead of seeming artificially difficult, these writers express an intellectual and emotional urgency so powerful that it bursts the bonds of convention. What they do seems right, appropriate, inevitable. They are so dazzling that other writers are often enticed to emulate them. But lesser writers who are hypnotized by technical ingenuity sometimes don't realize they have forfeited the warmth, the humanity, and the urgency that make fiction live. If your readers don't care what happens next, it doesn't make any difference how smart you are.

See *Documents / Diaries / Letters, Facade, Metafiction, Style*.

▼

TRANSITIONS

○ You often need to get your characters from one period of time to another, or from one place to another. Or you need to shift from one set of characters to another, or to move from one point of view to another. Such *transitions*, handled smoothly, do not disrupt the fictional world. Handled abruptly, they make readers conscious of the writing, and momentarily violate the fictional world.

Establishing action in time must be done clearly. Readers

need to know when actions occur in relation to other actions. The simplest transition occurs through the narrative voice. A scene ends, and the next paragraph begins, "The following Tuesday the bus arrived" or "They did not see each other until the next summer." The intervening time need not be dealt with at all. This keeps the narrative crisp and focused.

Until you make place clear, the writing has a kind of talking-heads feeling. A transition that opens with an image of where the characters are creates immediacy at once.

> I was gone for two years. When I walked up the drive, she was sitting on the porch as if she hadn't moved in all that time. She smiled lazily when she saw me. "Hey," she said, "catch any?"

A slightly more detailed transition succinctly gives the sense of the time that is being passed over. A major scene ends, and a couple of sentences bring readers to the next scene:

> Andrew spent the spring planting herbs that would not grow and reading books he could not finish. The first week in June she called. She would be waiting in front of the post office.

Merely skipping a space suggests a change of time and scene:

Or use an asterisk:

*

That's simple and succinct. The next section can be later in the day or in a different century. Your opening sentences can embed information so that your readers know where and when and with whom the new scene is taking place. Description, dialogue, thought, or physical action can accomplish that almost invisibly.

Transitions from place to place are similar to time transitions. A skipped space in the text tells readers that one scene has ended. The opening paragraph of the next scene establishes where the characters are and the transition is accomplished. If you want to say how a character got from place to place, just summarize. "Andrew drove the Renault down to the post office."

Transitions in point of view from one character to another can also be done in various ways. A skipped space or an asterisk, again. Some writers use dingbats. In *As I Lay Dying* Faulkner uses the name of the speaker as the title of each section. But usually the opening lines can be written so it's clear whose head you are in.

Going between characters within a single scene demands that you move fluidly. If you're deep within one character's head and abruptly switch to another character's head, it will be jarring.

Here are some methods to help you switch points of view. Establish in the opening that readers should expect the story to be told with multiple viewpoints. A sentence as simple as "Neither Greta nor Ben was happy about having to visit his mother's dog" gives you license to move into the minds of whomever you like. You can slide into a character's mind with a transitional sentence that describes the character doing something. If you add another sentence that has to do with perception the transition is clear and smooth. When you want to leave that character's head, come back out the same way, then slide into the next character. Seeing and touching play an important part in moving from one person to another.

> Agnes felt like screaming as she watched Dick playing with his fingernails. "Here," she said, handing him a pair of scissors. Dick scrutinized the scissors. There was a little flower pattern etched in the surface. They look Belgian, he thought. He looked at Agnes curiously.

Perhaps the clearest instruction comes from carefully reading a master like Flaubert. For example, in *Madame Bovary*, Emma yells at Charles, and in the next paragraph we are in Charles's head. Emma asks Leon to run an errand, and in the next paragraph we are in Leon's mind. Emma asks the notary for help, and in the next paragraph we are in the notary's thoughts. Flaubert shows how gracefully writers can move from consciousness to consciousness.

Dealing with transitions in time, space, and point of view might not fit in with the romantic notion of the Writer as Tortured Genius, but notice how deftly, how invisibly, the writers you admire handle such matters. The more you recognize their craftsmanship, the more fully you understand what you can learn.

See *Narrator, Point of View, Reading, Showing and Telling*.

▼

TRUST YOUR MATERIAL

o   You are interesting. Your experiences, your imagination, your perceptions, your emotions are interesting. What is closest to you is valuable for your art. Believe that.

Your honesty and your talent are inseparable. Don't falsify by conventionalizing. Your uniqueness lies not in fulfilling cultural stereotypes but in expressing what you really uncover, like it or not.

Here are some of the problems writers get into if they don't trust their material.

They rush. They don't believe that a detailed description of a woman frying corn fritters can be wonderful. So they just say it—they don't create the experience. Don't keep yourself from describing what you want for fear of boring your readers. If it was fascinating to you, it can fascinate them.

Some writers falsify their material. They think readers expect a certain version of reality, and though they have experienced it in a more complex way, they try to supply what they think they should. So, even though they have complicated, mixed feelings about the grandfather, they leave out the rude and the crude and give a censored version.

Or they go for sensationalism. Since they don't fully believe that the characters and their lives are intrinsically interesting, they put in something contrived or melodramatic.

See "Write What You Know."

VOICE

○ Voice is the writer's style as it is expressed in the characters' speech and thoughts.

Writers can be many people and can have access to many voices. They can assume the voice of an adolescent girl, an elderly woman, a bitter young boy, an incompetent salesman, an unhappy teacher. Each voice creates a character. The notion of *voice* is not hard to understand when it's clear that a character is telling a story in first person. Salinger's opening to *Catcher in the Rye* creates Holden Caulfield:

> If you really want to hear about it, the first thing you'll probably want to know is where I was born, and what my lousy childhood was like, and how my parents were occupied and all before they had me, and all that David Copperfield kind of crap, but I don't feel like going into it, if you want to know the truth.

Salinger is establishing Holden's speech rhythms, vocabulary, and degree of awareness—he's sharp, rude, young but insightful, and he reads books. That voice has to be consistent if it's going to be convincing. If Holden started sounding like a *New York Times* contributor, "I investigated various states of mind—madness, horror, hilarity—fully at ease in exploring every one," we say the character *breaks voice*.

Voice in third person is a bit more elusive. You are narrating, but not entirely in your own voice. Your reader hears your character's voice through you, and simultaneously hears you through your character. Carson McCullers begins *The Member of the Wedding:*

> It happened that green and crazy summer when Frankie was twelve years old. This was the summer when for a long time she had not been a member. She belonged to no club and was a member of nothing in the world. Frankie had become an unjoined person who hung around in doorways and, she was afraid.

As the book goes on, that direct, young voice with its breathless little *and*s lets us hear Frankie through McCullers. McCullers/Frankie describes the cook:

> Her hair was parted, plaited, and greased close to the skull, and she had a flat and quiet face. There was only one thing wrong about Berenice—her left eye was bright blue glass.

We won't hear McCullers/Frankie sound like this:

> It was full dark now, but still early; Gay Street was full of absorbed faces; many of the store windows were still alight. Plaster people, in ennobled postures, stiffly wore untouchably new clothes; there was even a little boy, with short, straight pants, bare knees and high socks, obviously a sissy: but he wore a cap, all the same, not a hat like a baby.

That's Rufus, the young boy in James Agee's *Death in the Family*. But it's Agee/Rufus, a kind of double voice with its own rules.

To stay in voice you have to hear that voice in your head. As you can see from the examples, writers establish a range of vocabulary, imagery, phrasing, and style of punctuation. Reading your story aloud is a fine way of testing your control of the voice. You'll hear where the voice has gone flat or lost its rhythm. You'll hear where a certain insight or piece of information seems out of character.

Don't accept the notion that the character could possibly say or think this or that. *Possibly* is not enough. You want that shock of recognition—you want your readers to say *Yes!*, not *Well, maybe*.

See *Character, Facade, Point of View, Style*.

▼

WORKSHOPS

o On the evening of the day that the first person thought up the idea of telling a story, he or she probably shouted the story around the fire. Friends and relatives congregated. One listener said the story made no sense. A cousin said he could just smell the bear's breath. Someone else said no one could throw a spear that far.

The form evolved to wigwams, wickiups, stoas, and brigantines. It happened in pubs, clubs, gardens, dens, parlors, and sewing rooms. Friends or relatives sat around and made comments, some sarcastic, some admiring, some helpful, and some plain stupid. Storytelling moved to bars and restaurants, newspaper backrooms, and editorial offices. And finally to classrooms and conference rooms, where these gatherings got called "workshops" and were immediately blamed for whatever was wrong with fiction.

Which brings us up to now, and to questions about your own relationship to fiction workshops. Are they good or evil? Do they help or hinder? What are their uses and what are their drawbacks?

Fiction workshops are generally organized so that writers can critique each other's work. The structure of the workshop gives you, first, a test audience. You see what flies and what doesn't. Second, the reactions and suggestions by your fellow writers are supposed to be helpful to you; they isolate problems and offer solutions. Third, the person who is organizing the workshop provides criticism from his or her own perspective.

In a good workshop, the test audience is fair, open-minded, and knowledgeable enough to appreciate a variety of writing. The participants accept the story on its own terms, whether it's about quilting, basketball, or alcoholism. They also understand that there are different ways to tell a story, and that each way has its own integrity. They read as all good readers read. They accept the spirit of the story, and then judge whether it fulfilled its own aspirations. They recognize achievement and generously acknowledge it. They notice problems and bring them up for discussion.

In a bad workshop the participants become blocked by their own reactions: "Oh, I hate sports stories," or "I don't want to read about sordid things." They aren't open to different ways of telling a story and insist that there is one right way. A bad workshop can be bad in many ways. If the participants are not sufficiently well read, they'll often praise sentimental, clichéd, and contrived stories, and will condemn fresh, innovative, and honest fiction. If the participants are too well read, they may become negative because the work at hand is not equivalent to something they recently saw in some journal that the writer "really ought to read."

Workshops can turn into mutual admiration societies, a relatively benign phenomenon in which everyone tells everyone else how wonderful they are. Though there's not much real criticism in these meetings, they keep people's spirits up and let writers grow at their own pace. The disadvantages in the long run are obvious. Writers who use such a workshop as a point of reference—"Everyone loved this story so much"—are puzzled or bitter when they are criticized or rejected by the outside world.

Workshops can also become mutual destruction associations, a more malign development in which each participant tries to convince the other members that they are incapable of writing fiction at all. These workshops can do real damage. The criticism is articulated with such ferocity and dogmatism that a beginning writer can be silenced for years. It's best to escape such groups as soon as possible.

Having said this, I believe the experience of fiction workshops is worth the risk. By putting your story up for discussion you learn how to listen to criticism and how to deal with it. By hearing the reactions to other stories you begin to recognize who in the workshop is perceptive, judicious, and balanced in judgment. Probably you should pay attention to those persons when your story is discussed. You recognize that the opinions of some people should be discounted. Some are negative bullies and others are uncritical enthusiasts. A person may vehemently attack some aspect of a story that isn't worth more than a minute of discussion because it could be cleared up with the insertion of a single sentence. Someone else may wax rhapsodic about what you recognize as contrived and dishonest. What if that person loves your story?

Remember that you are learning from these people. You're learning what to aspire to as a critic of others' work, what you do want to be, and what you don't want to be. You are learning to articulate your reactions to a story, to go beyond the feeling of "I don't like it" to an analysis of why it doesn't work and what it needs. And as you learn to do that for others' work you are teaching yourself to look at your own work with the same critical eye.

A good workshop will often result in useful reactions. "This character does not seem clear." "That scene was confusing." "The ending doesn't work." But it is easier to see problems than to solve them. The solutions that are suggested by the workshop are to be tasted gingerly and not swallowed whole. You need to sort them out and reflect on their usefulness. Other writers may be accurate in focusing on what's wrong, but their ideas on how to fix things can tell more about them than about you. Your hope for help can make you leap too eagerly at what may sound like plausible solutions. Stay loose and remember that useful suggestions sometimes come from unpredictable places.

A good workshop is guided rather than dominated by the person designated to be in charge. You should find a workshop run by a central person who has more experience and insight than the participants, who moves the discussion along, prevents various excesses, and adds useful commentary.

Good workshops can occur anywhere—in community centers, churches, colleges, and art associations. Friends organize their own workshops, meeting in living rooms, and keeping each other productive.

In some workshops, writers read their stories aloud. In others, everyone reads the stories before the meeting. Each method has its adherents. I think it works better to have stories read beforehand. That saves meeting time, and allows participants to mull over the stories. Some fine stories don't read aloud particularly well. The prose may be too rich, the time shifts complex, or the voices difficult to follow.

Some workshops allow the writer to explain the story as part of the discussion. This can be productive, but often a writer will defend his story, denying the validity of his critics' reactions. Embarrassing impasses can occur—someone says the character of Julia seems sexist, and the writer says it is not, that the critic has misunderstood. So what is the answer? My feeling is that since writers can't follow their stories around to explain what they really mean, doing that in a workshop is counterproductive. If the writer gets his audience to assent to what he intended rather than to what really is on the page, it's no victory for anybody. But all kinds of workshop formats have their own successes.

It's difficult to try to be a writer. Workshops can provide deadlines, criticism, encouragement, and give you a few useful callouses which will be helpful when you collect the inevitable rejection slips.

In that first workshop, the people sitting around the fire probably made some useful suggestions, and the teller of the story, though irritated that night, by the next day had decided to revise the ending.

See *Advice, Reading, Revision.*

▼

ZIGZAG

This term is useful for describing what might be called *micro-plotting.* Plot refers to what happens in the work as a whole—the upturns and downturns, the changing positions of the characters. For example, the plot outline for a piece of fiction might be as follows:

> Vilmar is happy and about to be married. Vilmar is arrested. He escapes. While on the run, he discovers who framed him. He is captured again, and is to be executed. At the trial he exposes the real villains. Vilmar is exonerated and wed.

Zigzagging is on a smaller scale. It involves producing tension within a single scene by creating fluctuations of feeling to maintain a high degree of attention.

For example, we read a sequence in which we believe Vilmar is going to kiss his sweetheart. But he's too shy to kiss her. No, he leans his face toward hers, but she turns her head away. She looks at him now, but he's afraid to try again. He's steeling himself to do it, but someone is coming. No, it's just the wind in the leaves. Now she is nervous, but Vilmar feels bold. The church bell rings forbiddingly. They both look up. Suddenly their lips meet.

Tension is created by this rhythm. The backs and forths, the advances and retreats all move toward a goal. The zigzag is a micro-paradigm of plotting.

You can exploit the excitement generated by zigzags in physical action as easily as the film director does in a chase or a fight sequence. Vilmar's escaped under the house! Good. But the gangster's dog is sniffing under the house! Oh no! But the dog finds a bone and ignores Vilmar! Good. But now the gangster is looking under the house! Uh oh! But Vilmar has rolled behind a log! Thank goodness. But it's covered with fire ants; he's going to have to make a run for it! And so on.

The most melodramatic and the most sophisticated of fictions share this heartbeat. Flaubert does it in his scenes with Emma as readers watch her mind dart from one impulse to another. A conversation in a Henry James novel, with its rhythm of understandings and misunderstandings, uses the same techniques for creating suspense as the adventures of Benji as he is pursued by his kidnappers. The last chapter of Hemingway's *A Farewell to Arms* plays on this micro-plotting device as we wonder whether Catherine and the baby will live or die.

Zigzagging reflects psychological reality—the way hopes and fears alternate, how in our desperation we leap at solutions that we quickly reject, how human situations can change drastically from one moment to the next. And for readers zigzagging makes each scene electric with suspense.

See *Intrigant, Position, Suspense, Tension.*

PART IV

READABLES: WHERE TO LEARN MORE

◯ Reading about writing isn't writing, of course. You already know that no book on fishing will bring home a trout, and no book on fiction will write your story. But there's pleasure as well as instruction in such reading. Books on writing fiction range from the inspirational to the technical, from encouraging you to climb the aesthetic Alps to advising you how to crack the commercial marketplace.

The books listed here address different problems. Some, like Kenneth Atchity's guide, have to do with managing and organizing your life to be a more productive writer. The works by Natalie Goldberg and Gabriele Rico stress exercises to free your imagination. Janet Burroway's detailed and thoughtful discussions help you to think about your own writing more clearly. John Gardner provides useful advice with an enthusiasm that helps keep your spirits up. Rust Hills's pithy comments are often helpful. William Sloane's elegant, tough-minded observations communicate the distillation of a lifetime of editorial experience.

Some books on the following list are about the pragmatics of publishing. They give direct, solid information about where you should send material and how to deal with magazines, book publishers, agents, editors, and contracts. They tell you everything from what your manuscript should look like to how to publish your own book.

Dictionaries, thesauruses, style books, and grammar handbooks are indispensable. No one book has all the answers to any interesting question about usage, style, vocabulary, or grammar. So collect them. You'll never regret your reference books.

Many of the books mentioned here have bibliographies that will lead you to other useful books. I'm including books I like, and books that don't often get mentioned but deserve to be, and books that are just too important to omit.

Anthony, Carolyn, ed. *Family Portraits: Remembrances by Twenty Distinguished Writers.* New York: Doubleday, 1989.
These autobiographical reminiscences all focus on a person who had a profound influence on each writer's life. They're not only interesting reading, but inspire a reexamination of your own past, to see how it nourished your writing.

Appelbaum, Judith, and Nancy Evans. *How to Get Happily Published.* New York: Harper & Row, 1978.

Full of sound, realistic information. This is useful for those writers who have only the vaguest notions of the needs and practices of the publishing industry. Although upbeat and positive, it makes clear that creating the manuscript is only one step in a complicated and chancy process.

Atchity, Kenneth. *A Writer's Time: A Guide to the Creative Process from Vision through Revision.* New York: Norton, 1986.

In focusing on organization Atchity helps to take the hocus-pocus out of getting writing done. He challenges you not to fantasize about the book you would write if only you had the time or the space or whatever, but instead to plan realistically to accomplish what you want to do.

Brande, Dorothea: *Becoming a Writer.* Los Angeles: Tarcher, 1981.

Originally written in 1934, this book is as inspiring now as it was over fifty years ago. Brande reminds you how much you need to trust yourself, that there is joy in tapping your own creativity.

Brown, Rita Mae. *Starting from Scratch: A Different Kind of Writer's Manual.* New York: Bantam, 1988.

Lively, inspirational, energizing pieces.

Bunnin, Brad, and Peter Beren. *The Writer's Legal Companion: How to Deal Successfully with Copyrights, Contracts, Libel, Taxes, Agents and Publishers, Legal Relationships, and Marketing Strategies.* Reading, Mass.: Addison-Wesley, 1988.

As the title suggests, this book covers much territory. Although it doesn't particularly focus on the problems of those who write fiction, it is a good, fast-moving introduction to the business end of writing, with useful advice on what may constitute invasion of privacy or defamation.

Burroway, Janet. *Writing Fiction: A Guide to Narrative Craft,* 3rd ed. Boston: Little, Brown, forthcoming (1991).
The classic, most widely accepted text. Clear, thoughtful, and well-written discussions will provide you with useful and invigorating advice. Story selections provide helpful examples, and suggestions and exercises provoke good ideas.

Burton, William C. *Legal Thesaurus.* New York: Macmillan, 1980.
A wonderful book, especially for devout ironists. Full of marvelously esoteric multisyllabic Latinate synonyms. Where else can you look up "deflagrate" as a main entry and find as a synonym "torrefy"?

Curtis, Richard. *How to Be Your Own Literary Agent.* Boston: Houghton-Mifflin, 1983.
A hardheaded, practical book that demystifies the publishing industry.

Forster, E. M. *Aspects of the Novel.* New York: Harcourt Brace, 1927.
Often reprinted, this slim classic is to fiction what Strunk and White's *Elements of Style* is to prose.

Gardner, John. *The Art of Fiction: Notes on Craft for Young Writers.* New York: Knopf, 1984.
Lively, useful, perceptive, and humane. As readable as a novel, as helpful as a handbook.

Gardner, John. *On Becoming a Novelist*. New York: Harper & Row, 1983.

Energy, encouragement, and good, solid advice for the long winding road of novel creation.

Goldberg, Natalie. *Writing Down the Bones: Freeing the Writer Within*. Boston: Shambhala, 1986.

Inspiring short essays on getting going, subjects, using emotions. Also specific technical advice given in an engaging, personal voice.

Goldfarb, Ronald L., and Gail E. Ross. *The Writer's Lawyer: Essential Legal Advice for Writers and Editors in All Media*. New York: Times Books, 1989.

This thoughtful handbook with its useful business information and lively accounts of recent legal cases is somewhat ominous for devotees of the First Amendment. Of particular importance are the chapters "Protecting Your Good Ideas," "What Every Writer Should Know about Libel," and "What Every Writer Should Know about Privacy."

Hills, Rust. *Writing in General and the Short Story in Particular: An Informal Textbook*. Boston: Houghton-Mifflin, 1977.

Useful, practical, cogent advice.

International Directory of Little Magazines and Small Presses. Len Fulton, ed. Pasadena: Dustbooks (annual).

Not only does this book have a huge number of entries, but each publisher or editor gives a useful, sometimes chatty, description of the needs of the press or magazine.

International Literary Market Place. New York: R. R. Bowker (annual).

The most efficient source of those elusive overseas

addresses for foreign publishers, presses, and literary organizations.

James, Henry. *The House of Fiction*. Leon Edel, ed. London: Hart Davis, 1957.

A collection of James's essays on the novel including the infinitely quotable "The Art of Fiction." He reminds you, as so many will after him, that "an ounce of examples is worth a ton of generalities."

Letters and journals. (Look up authors who interest you to see what collections are available.)

The collected letters of writers and editors not only make good reading, but also give a sense of the writer's life. In Max Perkins's letters to Hemingway or Flaubert's letters to Maupassant, you are struck by how much the interchanges sound like a contemporary writing workshop. Some writers speak only of money and others talk about their day's progress as if they were laying linoleum. But when they do mention writing, you find the sort of things you're likely to paste up on your wall. Kafka, for example, explains, "Writing is the most important thing in the world for me, as important as madness to a madman." Flaubert tells a friend in a letter, "Stupidity consists of wanting to reach conclusions." Chekhov answers an aspiring author who wants to know if he should continue to write, "If it gives you pleasure, and you can learn punctuation." Letter collections tend to be browseable forms of amusement in which, for better or worse, you can hear the writer's own voice.

Literary Market Place: The Directory of the American Book Publishing Industry. New York: R. R. Bowker (annual).

You might not want to buy this $100 paperback, but you ought to know exactly where it is in your local library. Updated annually, it lists addresses and phone numbers of agents, book clubs, contests, and hundreds of publishers, including 800 numbers for direct ordering. Its detailed listings will save you serious amounts of time.

Madden, David. *A Primer of the Novel: For Readers and Writers*. Metuchen, N.J.: Scarecrow, 1980.

A thoughtful book with a marvelous bibliography listing many works on writing from Chekhov and Proust to Roland Barthes and Ronald Sukenick.

Madden, David, and Richard Powers. *Writers' Revisions: An Annotated Bibliography of Articles and Books about Writers' Revisions and Their Comments on the Creative Process.* Metuchen, N.J.: Scarecrow, 1981.

Madden shows the incredible spectrum of methods that have been adopted by successful writers, and directs the reader to a dazzling array of opinions.

May, Charles E., ed. *Short Story Theories*. Athens, Ohio: Ohio University Press, 1976.

A collection of twenty essays by writers and critics attempting to define in one way or another what a short story is. The essays by writers like Frank O'Connor ("The Lonely Voice") and Eudora Welty ("The Reading and Writing of Short Stories") have useful comments. There's also a 25-page annotated bibliography showing that these arguments have been around for a long time.

The New Yorker (weekly publication).

New Yorker stories are often fresh, challenging, and

idiosyncratic, sometimes irritating and interminable, but the important feature is that the magazine is weekly—about 52 stories a year that will challenge, annoy, and instruct you.

There are other magazines that publish fine fiction: literary quarterlies such as *The Quarterly, Paris Review,* and *Antaeus;* quality monthlies like *Harper's* and *Atlantic;* and journals that are rarely seen on newsstands, such as *Ploughshares* and *Prairie Schooner.* Subscriptions not only put you in touch with interesting writing but also help support your own literary culture.

Novel and Short Story Writer's Market. Laurie Henry, ed. Cincinnati, Ohio: Writer's Digest Books (annual).

Formerly sold as the annual *Fiction Writer's Market.* Its virtue is that it lists many non-literary magazines that will also buy fiction. Good descriptions of each magazine's interests, requirements, and fees.

Publishers Weekly (weekly publication).

It's expensive to subscribe to, but virtually all libraries carry this trade magazine. *Publishers Weekly* is about sales, trends, and the marketplace economics of the book business. That can be discouraging for some, but it is an interesting world, and the interviews with writers (one in each issue) are often enlightening.

Reid, Ian. *The Short Story.* London: Methuen, 1977.

Admirably concise, intelligent discussion of taxonomy. Although this book is directed more toward critics than writers, you'll find that the distinctions Reid makes can help clarify your own ideas.

Rico, Gabriele Lusser. *Writing the Natural Way: Using Right Brain Techniques to Release Your Expressive Powers.* Los Angeles: Tarcher, 1983.

Lively exercises to encourage creativity and the discovery of self. Based on association techniques like clustering, creating trial webs, and discovering unifying threads, the book has led many people to discover more about themselves as writers. Its focus is on "enhancing creativity," so don't expect it to help you on technical and formal matters.

Rodale, J. I. *The Synonym Finder.* New York: Warner, 1978.

So useful, it's virtually a secret weapon. Unlike Roget's original quaint but complicated system, you simply look up a word, like "demolition," and find enough "pulverizing," "smashing," and "expunction" not only to give you the word you couldn't recall, but also to suggest ideas you hadn't thought of. Don't confuse it with Rodale's *The Word Finder,* which is sparse.

Sloane, William. *The Craft of Writing.* New York: Norton, 1979.

Graceful, charming, and wise. These are the thoughts of a highly respected editor who devoted his life to working with writers.

Sternburg, Janet, ed. *The Writer on Her Work.* Volumes I and II. New York: Norton, 1980, 1991.

In Volume I, sixteen American writers contribute essays dealing with how they work and what conspires to prevent them from working. Their energy, intelligence, and talent will send you back to the keyboard with fresh strength. A second volume of commissioned essays includes American writers and writers from other countries. Janet Sternburg contributes an introduction to each volume.

Strong, William S. *The Copyright Book: A Practical Guide,* 3rd ed. Cambridge, Mass.: M.I.T. Press, 1990.

Writers seem constantly confused about how copyright works. Some still believe the old 28-year renewable rule is still in effect. Others have a vague notion of changes but are hazy about the details. This concise, authoritative book clearly explains what is still governed by the old copyright laws, the effect of the massive 1978 revisions, and the important modifications since 1978. It tells how to secure rights and deals with such slippery notions as what is *not* copyrightable, "infringement," and "fair use."

Strunk, William, Jr., and E. B. White. *The Elements of Style.* New York: Macmillan, 1979.

You'd think every person in the English-speaking world would know of this little book by now. Would that this were so.

Ueland, Brenda. *If You Want to Write.* St. Paul: Graywolf, 1987.

Originally appearing in 1938, this lovely, elegant tribute to the imagination still has the power to move you to free "your thoughts and the genius that is in all of us."

Webster's New Dictionary of Synonyms. Springfield, Mass.: G. and C. Merriam, 1973.

I don't know why people don't recommend this to each other more often. Unlike a thesaurus, which simply lists words, this book explains and exemplifies the differences of connotation and usage between similar words, like *decry, depreciate, disparage, derogate, detract, belittle,* and *minimize.* In a world in which people seem relatively insensitive, callous, indurated, and incurious about language, it's important for writers to preserve the subtleties and nuances that enrich both our vocabulary and our meanings.

Welty, Eudora. *One Writer's Beginnings.* Cambridge, Mass.: Harvard University Press, 1984.
As Welty beautifully tells the story of her own career, she teaches through charming anecdotes and aphorisms.

The Writer (monthly publication).
Originally founded in 1887, this magazine still appears faithfully, with pithy and pointed articles suggesting ways to improve your writing.

Writers at Work: The Paris Review Interviews. New York: Viking.
Since 1958 *The Paris Review* has been collecting its interviews in book form. The Eighth Series appeared in 1988. These long discussions are readable, lively, and thoughtful reflections on writing by many of our finest authors.

Writer's Digest (monthly publication).
Since 1920 the magazine *Writer's Digest* has been offering advice, encouragement, and useful listings of markets and contests to writers. Articles tend to be upbeat, lively, and focused on solutions to particular problems that its authors have faced.

Writer's Digest Books (publisher).

The venerable publisher of the *Writer's Market* series has a sizable list of how-to books for writers. They tend toward direct, pragmatic advice, emphasizing good story-telling values that will help sell stories and articles. The titles on genre fiction, like *Writing the Modern Mystery, Writing Young Adult Novels, Writing Romance Fiction, Writing and Selling Science Fiction,* are especially helpful since sound advice there is not easy to find.

The Writing Business: A Poets and Writers Handbook. New York: Poets and Writers Press, 1985.

Good, solid information and judgment on everything from self-publishing to how to arrange readings. Includes recommended further reading on such subjects as contracts, agents, and wills for writers.

Young, James N. *101 Plots Used and Abused.* Boston: Writer, 1946 (rev. ed. 1961).

A cheerfully sadistic compendium of contrived, horribly familiar surprise-ending stories that have tortured fiction editors for decades. Wonderful to read aloud to friends to clear out a party.

Zinsser, William. *On Writing Well,* 4th ed. New York: Perennial Library, 1990.

Although the book's subtitle is *An Informal Guide to Writing Nonfiction,* fiction writers will find Zinsser's principles for good prose consistently valuable. "Writing About a Place," "Trust Your Material," and "Humor" are especially rewarding. As Zinsser says in warning about being wishy-washy: "Don't be kind of bold. Be bold."